ABUNDANT JOY JUICE

Squeezed from God's Word

Joyce J. Ashley

Copyright © 2011 by Joyce J. Ashley

Abundant Joy Juice
Squeezed from God's Word
by Joyce J. Ashley

Printed in the United States of America

ISBN 9781619046597

All rights reserved solely by the author. The author guarantees all contents are original and do not infringe upon the legal rights of any other person or work. No part of this book may be reproduced in any form without the permission of the author. The views expressed in this book are not necessarily those of the publisher.

Unless otherwise indicated, Bible quotations are taken from The HOLY BIBLE, NEW INTERNATIONAL VERSION. NIV. Copyright © 1973, 1978, 1984, 2011 by International Bible Society. Used by permission of Zondervan; The New American Standard Bible. Copyright © 1960, 1962, 1963, 1968, 1971, 1972, 1973, 1975, 1977, 1995 by The Lockman Foundation; The New Century Version. Copyright © 1987, 1988, 1991 by Word Publishing, a division of Thomas Nelson, Inc.; The Amplified Bible. Copyright © 1954, 1958, 1962, 1964, 1965, 1987 by The Lockman Foundation; The *Holy Bible*, New Living Translation. Copyright © 1996 by Tyndale

House Publishers, Inc., Wheaton, Illinois 60189; The King James Version of the Bible; The New King James Version. Copyright © 1982 by Thomas Nelson, Inc.; and *The Message*. Copyright © 1993, 1994, 1995, 2000, 2001, 2002 by Eugene Peterson. Used by permission of NavPress Publishing Group.

www.xulonpress.com

Thank You

✳

Special thanks to my wonderful editor, Jennifer Hanchey, for her patience and willingness to, once again, help with my writing project. From start to finish, she has been a joyful partner whom I have grown to love and trust.

Jennifer lives in Franklin, Tennessee, with her husband, Brad, and their three beautiful children, Charlie, Lou, and Elijah.

FORWARD

✻

I first met Joy, Joy, JOYce, as I always call her, when she asked ME, a grieving mother who had lost a child a year and a half prior, to speak at a conference at her home church on the topic of JOY! At first I thought, "This lady has lost her marbles!" But then I started to think that Joyce Ashley was a genius. If *I* could still possess joy in my soul, then ANYONE can! I began to pray about whether or not God was calling me to the "EnJOY the JOurneY" Women's Conference in Douglas, Georgia…and sure enough, He was!

I began digging into God's Word for passages on joy and recalling how God had used scripture to remind me in those first few desperate months after my youngest son, Bronner, had journeyed into Heaven, that "no one can take my joy from me, for Jesus is my joy and His joy makes me strong." (paraphrased from John 16:22 and Nehemiah 8:10; *Scripture Confessions for Kids* by Harrison House)

All of this research turned out to be just what was needed to continue to lift my spirit out of what could have easily turned into despair after such a devastating tragedy. I knew God was using my son's Heaven-going (I never use the word "death" because I believe Bronner is more alive than any of us living on the Earth; he lives with the Author of Life and the Perfecter of Our Faith, Jesus, in the Land of the Living, the Kingdom of Light) to bring others to Himself. But even when you understand the why, the separation of a mother from her baby is never easy. So, studying joy in the midst of grief turned out to be a huge blessing for me personally, and I thank Joy, Joy, JOYce for being "as wise as a serpent" but as joyful as…well… herself.

She truly is one of the most joyful people I have ever met and that comes through in this devotional, ***Abundant Joy Juice, Squeezed from God's Word***. In asking me to speak at a conference on joy, Joyce Ashley demonstrated her obvious understanding of where true joy comes—in knowing the Lord. Joyce knows that happiness comes and goes, but joy is much deeper. For me it appears more as peace that transcends all understanding and hope for the future, but it also shows itself in the fact that I can be happy even if I had bury my 2 ½ year old son on a rainy January day in 2008. Not only can I stand firm in my faith but I can also laugh. I can laugh at a comedian, of all things, and I have. I can laugh at something silly one of my boys does, and I can laugh "at the time to come" (Proverbs 31:25) because I know it will include one joyous reunion with my precious son and a glorious face to face encounter with my Lord and Savior and embraces with both.

God's favorite teaching method is story telling. Joyce Ashley has a story to tell—of joy. She has deep wisdom to impart that comes across in the stories of her everyday life. She lives out the joy of the Lord daily, hourly, and truly, moment by moment, for that is the only way to keep steadfast in any aspect of our walk with the Lord. Keep in mind that doesn't mean Joyce never gets sad. She does. But whatever her circumstance, she can dig deep into the well of her soul where there resides the Holy Spirit of God who helps her, who strengthens her and reminds her that she is a child of the King of Kings and the Lord of Lords.

My circumstance is that I need more help than maybe someone else does to keep myself focused on living out the joy of the Lord, so I was thankful when Joyce sent me her manuscript to read over the summer. It was helpful to me to get up and read her words and be reminded, once again, that "no one can take my joy from me, for Jesus is my joy and His joy makes me strong." I think all of us need to be reminded of this from time to time and usually even daily. I hope you will use **Abundant Joy Juice** as a daily devotional to keep in step with this immensely important fruit of the Spirit, that you may walk in the joy that is available to all of us through the Holy Spirit of God.

With love,
Sherri Burgess
Wife of Rick Burgess, Co-Host of the Rick and Bubba Radio Show

Endorsements

✷

Joyce Ashley's words in *Abundant Joy Juice* are a fresh-squeezed delight that both nourish the heart and strengthen the soul. Join her as through the pages of this book she inspires, encourages and points you to the Lord. With relevant topics and practical insights into the One who desires for you to experience joy beyond measure, this book will teach you to daily drink deep of His infinite wisdom and lavish love.

Karen Ehman
Proverbs 31 Ministries National Director of Speakers
Author of *A Life That Says Welcome* **and** *The Complete Guide to Getting and Staying Organized.*

It is my joy to endorse Joyce Ashley's new devotional book ***Abundant Joy Juice***. This book is a treasury of short and meaningful devotionals for busy women who want to have that time with God. Joyce's insight and sense of humor are a refreshing and great way to start or end you day. Her illustrations taken from her own life experiences make you laugh and are a great comfort to know that we as women share a myriad of the same experiences. Joyce's book will forever remain part of my library, catalogued under encouragement, of course!

Cindy Evers
Pastor's Wife and Women's Ministry Coordinator
Northside Baptist Church, Tifton, GA

My list of frustrations can grow long: finances, a house I can't keep clean, children with childish choices, too many items on my to-do list and so on. When I park my mind on these things, discouragement fills my heart. But God has another option:

Joy. That's oh-so easy to say, but much harder to live out. That's why I loved Joyce Ashley's book, *Abundant Joy Juice.* Joyce doesn't just tell you to be joyful, she actually equips you with the Word of God, biblical truth, and some hard-earned wisdom that every woman can relate to. Joyce's book reads like a friend is sharing her life with you, and when you are done you feel loved, re-energized and ready to be filled with God's joy. Whether you are going through a tough time, or just need a bit of encouragement, *Abundant Joy Juice* will help focus your mind on God's gift of joy – and we all need more of that!

Glynnis Whitwer
Writer and editor, Proverbs 31 Ministries
Author, "I Used to Be So Organized"

DEDICATION

✳

My first book, ***Joy Juice: Delightful Flavors of JOY in the Lord***, was such an exciting endeavor for me...the fulfillment of a life-long dream. The people of my community and friends throughout the country were instruments of encouragement as they helped me celebrate the birth of that first book project. Soon after publication, I began to hear, "When are you going to write the next one?" God used those validating words to motivate me to embark, once again, on another writing journey which led to this second devotional book about God's joy.

Abundant Joy Juice, Squeezed from God's Word is dedicated to my many friends. I consider you to be God's gifts of encouragement in my life. There are too many special friends to list by name, but you know who you are. What a blessing you've been in my life! Indeed, God has poured out His joy into my heart through rich relationships, which are much more valuable than material wealth. Thank you, dear friends—for loving me, believing in me and for encouraging me to pursue God's purpose in my life. Never forget that you are a great source of joy to me, and I count each of you as a treasure that God has lavished on me in love.

Shouts of joyful praise go to my precious family. My supportive husband, who is affectionately known these days as Papa Pat, continues to be the love of my life and my chief cheerleader. I cannot imagine doing life without him. Thank you for sharing this life of abundant joy with me, Pat. The best is yet to come!

To our children and GRANDchildren, who make me laugh often and feel loved always, I say, "God has blessed me, indeed! I praise the Lord for you and the exuberant joy that is ours because of His blessings. As our family continues to grow, each new addition brings a special element of joy. Being a wife, mother, and a "GiGi" are the most joyful roles that I've played in this script called Life. Thank you for being God's vessels of joy to me personally."

To my mother, brother, sister, and extended family members, I express my gratitude for the laughter and joy that we've shared through the years. MeMa, you have been and continue to be such a godly example to us all. Keep smiling and reminding us to ***"count it all joy."* (James 1:2)**

Though my daddy is now joyfully reaping his heavenly rewards, I must dedicate this book to him, as well. You will see in the following pages that I mention him often as being one of my joyful role models. What a blessing he was to so many! His joy-filled legacy lives on.

All glory and honor to our loving Heavenly Father who continues to pour out His Joy Juice into my life. He has filled me so full that I am compelled to overflow onto the pages of this book, praising Him for opportunities to share a double portion of His joy with others. May each one who reads it *"welcome the message with the joy given by the Holy Spirit"* **(1 Thess. 1:6b).**

Table of Contents

✷

Introduction xxiii

Chapter One: A Gulp of Glorified Joy Juice 27

Chapter Two: Generously Give Giant Servings of Joy Juice 61

Chapter Three: Abundant Joy Juice 95

Chapter Four: Children Love Joy Juice 127

Chapter Five: Hidden Recipes for Joy Juice 159

Chapter Six: Dreaming of Joy Juice 189

Chapter Seven: Household Uses for Joy Juice 217

Chapter Eight: Garden-grown Joy Juice 243

Chapter Nine: Joy Juice: It's Simply Divine! 273

Chapter Ten: Pride and Jealousy: NOT a
 Recipe for Joy Juice 301

Chapter Eleven: Tunes and Tales of Joy Juice 331

Chapter Twelve: Joy Juice Droplets of
 Prayer and Grace 363

Introduction

✳

"Rejoice always; pray continually; give thanks in all circumstances, for this is God's will for you in Christ Jesus."
(1 Thessalonians 5:16-18)

Several months after my radio ministry was off and running, a gentleman commented that he wondered when I'd run out of joy verses and things to say about the subject of joy. Since I was at the beginning of the *Joy Juice* journey, I found myself thinking he'd made a rather good point. However, as I've studied the Scripture and written literally hundreds of devotionals on the subject of the biblical fruit of joy, I've discovered that there is no end to the joy of the Lord. No matter where I turn in the Bible, it doesn't take long before I can see the love of God. And, with His love, there is joy.

The world's definition of joy is very different from the biblical meaning. Many people think that joy is the same as happiness. Not true! There have been countless times that I've not been happy, yet I've still felt the peace and joy of the Lord in the midst of these hard times. May I give you a personal example?

Several years ago, my beloved daddy was extremely ill. A dear friend of the family came to visit him in the hospital. She had been at the feet of Jesus that morning and was strongly prompted by the Holy Spirit to put everything aside that day and make a trip to the hospital to visit my daddy. (She told us later about the urgency she sensed.)

My daddy and she had a special relationship because they both loved the Lord and shared the gift of music. They had sung together through the years in church services, at funerals and for other special events. On that particular day, this precious friend obeyed God's leading and came to the hospital for a divine assignment. As she entered the room, she moved close to my dad's hospital bedside, took his hand in hers, and spoke to him with a huge, beautiful smile on her face and in her voice. The whole room immediately brightened.

She called my daddy's name and asked, "Would you sing with me this morning? Let's sing 'Amazing Grace.'" A distinct sparkle returned to his eyes and he quickly agreed; the two of them began to sing. Never will I forget the sweet melody of their voices blending together in praise to the Savior.

My mom and I sat in the corner of the room in awe, for we knew we were witnessing a God-appointed moment. The presence (and power) of God was evident. You see, Daddy had not been able to think clearly or breathe without struggling for days. His ability to communicate was nearly nonexistent at that point. Yet God touched his body one last time and strengthened him for these few, joyful moments. He was able to remember every word of every verse of the old hymn. And he had breath enough to sing strongly and passionately.

Tears were flowing down my mom's cheeks and mine. We were being blessed with a joyful miracle. It was evident that Daddy's days were numbered; for that, we were sad. Yet, in this moment of utter despair, there was peace and joy because we knew that God was in control. He demonstrated His love with this unexpected serving of joy in the midst of our sorrowful time.

Daddy went home to be with the Lord the very next day. But that cherished memory of his praising the Lord in song—even on his death bed—will be with us for the rest of our lives. Our God is a good, loving, faithful God. In *every* situation we can find His joy.

In the pages of this book, my hope is to share with you instances of joy in a variety of situations. May these short devotional messages sink deep into your heart so that His joy will be there for you when you need it most. Remember to ***"draw near to God and He will draw near to you"*** **(James 4:8, NASB).**

Chapter One

✻

A Gulp of Glorified Joy Juice

Have you had your Joy Juice today? Are you feeling joyful?

We don't always have that joyful feeling, do we? Sometimes, we feel downright grumpy. There may be some people who have listened to my radio broadcasts and/or read my devotionals on joy and thought, "That lady is always happy. She must be on drugs!"

Put your mind at ease. Nobody can be happy all the time—not even the Joy Juice lady. However, I am convinced that we *can* always have joy. Each of us has access to a 'joy fix' right at our fingertips; it's called a relationship with Jesus.

Let's think for a minute about what joy is *not*. Having the joy of the Lord is not the same thing as having a life free from problems. God has never promised that kind of ease; however, He has promised to be with us through the trials of life.

Remember **2 Corinthians 11: 24-27** in which Paul tells of his many challenges? Those verses confirm the following:

- Five times he received thirty-nine lashes.
- Three times he was beaten with rods.
- He was stoned.
- Three times he was shipwrecked.
- He was often in danger of robbers, of his own countrymen, and of the Gentiles.
- He suffered hardship and sleeplessness, hunger and thirst, cold and nakedness.

Wow! Can you imagine living such an eventful life? All of these things Paul actually experienced—and then some. Yet he wrote the letter to the Philippians, which is filled with references to joy. As a matter of fact, it has become known as the "book of joy". Because of his unwavering faith in God, Paul could practice joy in the midst of all those terrible circumstances.

Let's do a self-check to determine if we can do the same. Look inward, and ask God to peel away the layers so that you can see with clear spiritual vision. Intimate relationship with Christ is the only way to always find true, genuine joy.

Prayer: *Father, help me to remember that You are the Lord of joy. Please remove the scales from my eyes, and help me to see what is keeping me from being as close to You as I should be. As the old hymn says, "Open my eyes that I may see glimpses of truth thou hast for me."* [1]

Have you had your Joy Juice today? It really helps to be filled up with the joy of the Lord when tough times come your way.

None of us like to experience heartache and trouble. But the fact is that life is full of problems and trials. Some people have the false notion that when they accept Christ, they will be immune to major problems. They think God owes them a perfect life. However, that's not what the Bible teaches. We are to *"rejoice in the Lord always,"* as **Philippians 4:4** instructs, but that doesn't mean that we will always be in a state of euphoria.

Author James A. Kitchens writes that there are two major types of joy: internal joy and external joy. Internal joy comes from within, from a heart filled with the love of Christ; external joy comes and goes with whatever is happening on the outside, in our environment. When the circumstances change, our emotions tend to follow. [2]

If we are filled up on the inside with the love and joy of the Lord, then regardless of what's happening on the outside, we can cling to our relationship with Him. Though we may not feel happy, we can still *"be joyful in hope"* as **Romans 12:12** says. So, concentrate on your relationship with the Master Hope-Giver. You'll discover that He offers unlimited servings of Joy Juice.

Prayer: *Thank you, dear God, that I can have hope in You. Remind me of the promises throughout Your Word which teach that I can always trust in You. When the storms of life blow into my day and I begin to feel stressed and anxious, fill me with Your hope and joy. I thank You for my internal joy that comes from having a personal relationship with You. May that internal joy become eternal. Oh, what a glorious time that will be—to spend eternity with You!*

Have you had your Joy Juice today? You don't feel like drinking it? Well, please drink it anyway!

So often we base our decisions on our feelings. Faith, however, should never be about feelings. It's a conscious decision. It's kind of like "will-power," but I like to call it "God-power." When we go on a diet and are trying hard to lose a few pounds, we have to make a conscious decision to eat only what's healthy. We don't feel like cutting out those tasty foods that we enjoy so much; but if we want to reach our goal of shedding those pounds, we have to be determined to make the right choices.

The same is true of choosing joy. Joy does not come automatically. One has to make a decision to be joyful, and success has a lot to do with one's thought life. What kind of thoughts do you entertain? Do you choose to listen to gossip and criticism? Are you nursing a grudge? What about the movies you are watching and the books you are reading? Are they helping you to grow in your relationship with the Lord, or are they pulling you in the opposite direction?

Philippians 4:8 reminds us of what should be our focus:

Finally, brothers and sisters, whatever is true, whatever is noble, whatever is right, whatever is pure, whatever is lovely, whatever is admirable—if anything is excellent or praiseworthy—think about such things.

Drinking your Joy Juice is a sure way to keep your mind focused on the right things, and when you're focusing on the right things, you will experience the joy of the Lord.

Prayer: *Today, I choose joy! Father, help me to make a conscious effort throughout my day not to get caught up in the moment or the problem at hand. Rather, bring to mind this verse in Philippians and help me to dwell only on what is true, noble, right, pure, lovely, admirable, excellent, and praiseworthy. I can't do it without You. I need You to help me be joyful—even when I don't feel like it.*

Have you had your Joy Juice today? If you share this juice with others, then you're a joy-giver—and that's a good thing!

Mary Southerland tells a story about a young Christian seeking joy:

I once heard a story that offers a great prescription for joy. A young believer came to a man who had followed Christ for many years with this complaint. 'I have lost my joy!' the young man said. The older, wiser Christian responded, 'Go out and do something for someone else. Then repeat that act of kindness nine times. Then you will find joy!' [3]

Isn't this the kind of attitude Jesus modeled? **Matthew 20:28** says, *"The Son of Man did not come to be served, but to serve."* If we are serious about striving to be like Jesus, then we will follow his example of loving and serving. When we find ourselves in the habit of serving, we will discover a joy bubbling forth from deep inside us. And do you know where that joy originates? It comes from the heart of God.

Going back to Mary Southerland's words on being a joy-giver, consider another of her observations:

God stands today, arms open wide, ready to pour out His unspeakable gift of joy into our lives so that we can have joy; so that we can share that joy with others. Our gift back to Him is to be a joy-giver. The more you give, the more joy you will experience. The more joy you have, the more you will want to give—-but you cannot out-give God. He rewards 'joy-givers.' [4]

Think back over the past few days. Can you think of times you have given joy to someone, even once? Whether or not you are generous with your joy-giving, remember we never meet our quota. So pause and ask the Lord to pour a bucket full of joyful opportunities on you today and in the days to come. Follow His example: **"[He] *did not come to be served, but to serve.*"**

Prayer: *I am sliding my hand into Yours, dear Father. Intertwine your fingers with mine and give me the faith to trust You to show me who and how to serve today. May my spiritual ears be tuned to Your voice as You whisper words of direction into my heart. Make clear to me the plan You have in order that I may become a generous joy-giver.*

Abundant Joy Juice

Have you had your Joy Juice today? Even if you got up on the "wrong side of the bed" this morning, you need to drink in the joy of the Lord.

Are you convinced that joy doesn't always come naturally? Most of us don't wake up cheerfully every morning with a song in our heart—no matter how much we'd like to. We know that not one of us is immune to the problems of life. Be aware that there is an enemy out there that's trying to tempt us and misguide us at every turn.

The joyful truth, however, is that our God is stronger than the enemy. And if we are in right relationship with Jesus, then He will give us His strength to overcome the temptations and to make the right choices. **1 John 4:4** articulates this truth: ***"The one who is in you is greater than the one who is in the world."***

It is so important that we stay filled with the Greater One by studying the Bible and spending time with God in prayer. Yes, even when we don't feel like it. We should focus our thoughts on all that is good (and of God) so that we can overflow with the peace and joy that comes from sharing a relationship with Him.

Be reminded often that joy is not about a life free of problems. Rather, it's God's peace and assurance in the midst of heartache and disappointment. Joy is not all laughter and no sadness. It's God's arms wrapping around us as He wipes away our tears. Joy is not an endless reserve of physical energy; we all grow weary and tired. Joy is about resting in the Lord and trusting Him to take care of us.

Prayer: *"The one who is in you is greater than the one who is in the world." As I go throughout my day, I ask that this verse be brought to my memory over and over again. Especially when I sense an attack from the enemy, may I draw strength from the truth of this scripture, Father. Thank You for always being there for me and fighting my battles along side of me. Give me wisdom and joy to face the day.*

Have you had your Joy Juice today? It's in God's plan that we drink it faithfully.

Do you ever wonder about God's plan for your life? You do know, don't you, that you were created for a purpose? God didn't form you and me accidentally or because He was bored and didn't have anything better to do. We are all a part of His Master plan. We are told of his special plan for each person in **Jeremiah 1:5**: *"Before I made you in your mother's womb, I chose you. Before you were born, I set you apart for a special work"* **(NCV)**.

Have you figured out your special assignment—your purpose for life? Let me help you. In a nutshell, it's to glorify God in all that you do. Because we are all unique with different personalities, different abilities and interests, different strengths and weaknesses, our individual purposes will take on different looks. Each of us, however, should strive for the same the goal: to glorify God!

Many times we feel inadequate when we compare ourselves to others. We think we could never measure up, so why even try? Let me put your mind at ease. We are not supposed to be in competition with one another when it comes to serving God. We are "in this thing together" as Gerbert used to sing to my children on the Sandi Patti CD. [5]

God uses each one of us as a piece of the larger puzzle. We are all shaped differently to complete his plan. Like puzzle pieces, some of us are oddly shaped, some have distinct attributes, some have smooth edges, and some take a little longer to figure out where they go, but we all come together to make a beautiful picture of His love, grace, and, of course, joy.

Prayer: *Thank You for being my Creator. When You made me, You had a special plan in mind. Don't ever let me forget this truth. Guide me as I discover that plan, one puzzle piece at a time. Give me patience and determination not to force the pieces according* *to how I think they should fit, but let me trust You to show me where each odd part snugly and perfectly belongs. On days when it seems I'll never see the final picture, fill me with Your peace and comfort, and remind me of Your unconditional love and perfect timing.*

Abundant Joy Juice

Have you had your Joy Juice today? It will help get you ready for the ministry God has prepared for you.

Each of us who are Christians has been called to ministry. Don't panic! I don't mean that all of us will be preachers, teachers, or staff members at a church somewhere. We're not all gifted with the same skills and passions. But we *are* all called to minister to others in our own unique ways. We just have to be plugged in, listening to God as He speaks to our hearts and leads us.

A while ago, I plugged in my iron and gave it a few minutes to warm up. When I thought it was hot, I began to iron the shirt that my hubby needed the next day. It was soon evident that my efforts weren't making any difference in the appearance of that shirt. So I tested the iron like my mom had taught me years ago, being careful not to burn myself. Well, I need not have worried about it burning my finger. The iron was stone cold. I glanced to make sure it was plugged in; yes, it was. I began to fret and stew about how I was going to get those wrinkles out of our clothes. I was certain that my iron had died, bit the dust, and gone to the small appliance heaven.

After a few frustrated moments, I decided to examine the outlet once more. I made an enlightening discovery. The previous night we'd had company, and in a quick clean-up job, I'd set my crock pot on the laundry room floor. Instead of plugging in my iron that morning, I'd picked up the cord to my crock pot instead. All I needed to do was to plug in the right cord, and my iron worked perfectly.

How many times have I fretted and worried because I didn't think God was working like I thought He should? But, all along, He was right there, just as powerful as ever. I was the one who had not been plugged in to the right Power Source. **2 Samuel 22:33** expresses this thought perfectly: *"God is my strength and power: and he maketh my way perfect"* **(KJV)**.

Prayer: *Father, You are my Power Source. Why do I sometimes forget that? I find myself often tackling my day, my problems, and my projects in my own strength when it would be so much better if I would stop and put it all in Your hands. Remind me that my circumstances are not mine, but all Yours. Prick my heart continually to plug in to You, the mightiest of all power sources, and the One who leads to joy.*

Abundant Joy Juice

Have you had your Joy Juice today? It comes in a variety of flavors. Find the one that suits your taste.

God loves variety; that's obvious. Look around you! At every turn, you see diversity. No two people are alike (not even twins). There are countless varieties of flowers, trees, and plants which add to the beauty of nature. Even the clouds in the sky and billions of snowflakes that fall all over the world are each unique in their formation.

Because of his love for variety, God has created you and me for a special purpose. He has gifted us with special abilities for serving Him. These gifts are given to us, not because we have earned them or deserve them but because of His great love for each of us. He has uniquely and personally gifted each of us.

1 Corinthians 12:11 speaks of gifts: *"All these [gifts, achievements, abilities] are inspired and brought to pass by one and the same [Holy] Spirit, Who apportions to each person individually [exactly] as He chooses" (AMP).*

Abundant Joy Juice

We don't get to pick and choose our gifts. It's not like asking for what we want for our birthday or making a Christmas wish list. God gives us what He knows we need to fulfill His plan and His purpose. We should thank Him for giving us the gifts He has lovingly selected, and we must realize that we have a responsibility to use and polish those gifts. We must also remember that we can take no credit for what God has freely given us. All glory should go to Him!

So as you celebrate your God-given gifts, drink your special flavor of Joy Juice. Always be willing to share with those He brings into your path as He accomplishes His purpose through you.

Prayer: *Master, Creator, Majestic God, thank you for uniquely forming me in my mother's womb and giving me special gifts to use for Your glory. On those days when I get discouraged and can't see my gifts, please help me to be able to look past my inadequa-*

cies and focus on You and Your plan for my life. Give me an extra measure of joy on the days that I want to compare myself to others, reminding me that I am special in Your eyes. Thank You for loving me, just as I am. But, thank you for loving me so much that You will not allow me to stay where I am in my relationship with You. Draw me closer and closer and closer.

Have you had your Joy Juice today? Hope you plan to have plenty on hand for the upcoming weekend.

Most of us really look forward to weekends. It's a time to make plans for family, fun, or relaxation. Often our plans include catching up on chores or tackling a project that we've not had time to work on during the busy week. All of us make plans—whether they are spontaneous or meticulously thought out. But are we so caught up in our own plans that we forget that God has a master plan for our lives?

What is His master plan? Does anyone really know? We each have a specific purpose, but God's master plan is based on the fundamental concepts of love, faith, and grace.

In **Matthew 22:37-39** Jesus taught the following:

'Love the Lord your God with all your heart and with all your soul and with all your mind.' This is the first and greatest com-

mandment. And the second is like it: 'Love your neighbor as yourself.'

If we can get these two commandments right, then the other things will fall into place. To love God supremely should be our hearts' desire. When loving God is our main goal, we will be in continual pursuit of His plans and His purposes for our lives. And with that single-mindedness comes faith and acceptance of His grace in our daily walk.

In his sermon "Improving Your Serve," Pastor John Tucker quotes Albert Schweitzer: *"The only really happy people are those who have learned how to serve."* [6] To put that in the spiritual perspective, think of this: When we love God and live according to His plan, our hearts and lives will be overflowing with the joy of the Lord.

Prayer: *Help me to love You with all my heart and with all my soul and with all my mind, Lord. Even* *when others are rude and unlovable, give me Your strength to love them as You love them. If serving is what brings joy and delight to my life, then use me to serve as You see fit!* ***"Here am I. Send me"*** **(Isaiah 6:8).**

Abundant Joy Juice

Have you had your Joy Juice today? It's a must if you want to experience true joy.

Ever notice that some people are always optimistic and upbeat, no matter what's going on in their lives? Then there are others who are chronically pessimistic and critical. We all have times when it seems that the rug has been jerked right out from under us, but we still have a choice about how we land. Will we crash, or will we be determined to keep standing with the help of God?

We can choose to fall headlong into disappointment and despair, enjoying our misery and wanting everyone to know about it. Or we can choose to allow God to cushion the blow by catching us before we hit bottom. I'm not saying that our faith will keep us from heartache and difficulties. What I am sure of, however, is that we can trust our Savior to be just that—our Savior! Complete trust in Him will give assurance that Jesus will be there to catch us when life takes us by surprise. That's what James was talking about when he wrote, *"Consider it pure joy, my brothers and sisters, whenever you face trials of many kinds"* **(James 1:2).**

Remember that happiness and joy are not the same. To guarantee joy in our life, we must trust in the Savior who is an expert in catching us and holding us up. His arms are strong and loving—a place of peace, comfort, and true joy in all circumstances.

Rest in the security of Jesus' arms as you drink your Joy Juice faithfully. And remember, it pleases Him greatly when we share His love and joy with others.

Prayer: *Jesus, Precious Jesus! You are always there to catch me, hold me, and comfort me. For that truth I praise You and thank You. On those days that are not filled with happiness and laughter, please remind me that I can* **still *"consider it pure joy"*** *because of my relationship with You. Today, I choose to rest in the security of Your loving arms. What a joyful place to be!*

Abundant Joy Juice

Have you had your Joy Juice today? Be prepared for your day by bringing along an extra serving or two.

One thing's for sure, when we wake up each morning, we never know what life might bring. We may receive good news—maybe a new baby is on the way or someone got engaged or a loved one gets a great doctor's report. On the other hand, we may have the wind knocked out of us by devastating news such as a tragic accident or a terminal diagnosis. It could be the heartbreak of a marriage falling apart.

Though we can't see into the future, we know the One Who holds our future. This thought reminds me of the beautiful old hymn "Because He Lives." I can almost hear my beloved daddy bellowing out the words as he sang from the depths of his heart and soul—words that he believed with his entire being and taught his family by example. The chorus expresses why we can have joy in any trouble:

Because He lives, I can face tomorrow.
Because He lives, all fear is gone.

Because I know He holds the future,
And life is worth the living just because He lives. [7]

If I could add my own twist to this beautiful chorus, it might go something like this:

Because He lives, I can have JOY regardless,
Because He loves, my JOY is complete.
Because He longs for a relationship with me,
Life is abundantly JOYful and, oh, so wonderfully sweet!

Prayer: *No matter what life brings today, Lord, help me to trust You. Whether I receive bad news or good, empower me to give You praise. May I have a song in my heart—a song of joy. Because You live,* **I can** *face whatever comes my way. Thank You, Father, for this assurance and Your faithfulness.*

Abundant Joy Juice

Have you had your Joy Juice today? Children love to drink it!

Years ago, when our children were small, I was trying to study my Sunday School lesson that I had to teach the following Sunday. The children were supposed to be playing quietly in the next room. I had hardly begun to study when the first interruption came and then another and other. Exasperated with them I said, "I want you to go play and let me study! The next one who interrupts is going to be in big trouble!"

They dropped their little heads and started out of the room. But before they were completely out of sight, one turned around and bravely asked, "What's your Sunday School lesson about this week, Mommy?"

"It's about patience! Now, go play!"

As soon as the words were out of my mouth, I realized that God was speaking through these innocent children to teach *me* a life lesson. Was I demonstrating the patience and grace to my children that I was going to teach others about on Sunday? It was apparent that I had failed this test. I thought about all the times that God had been patient with me. Yet, here I was, not willing to do the same for these precious children who were gifts from God. What a pitiful example I was being!

It was at that point that I closed my book and Bible until after my children were asleep. I joined them for some mommy time. I was reminded of the verse in **Psalm 127: 3** that says, *"Children are a heritage from the LORD, offspring a reward (a gift) from him."* Parents, let's remember that spending time with our children speaks volumes to them, and it demonstrates the joy of the Lord. Strive to be a consistent, shining example of His love and joy—no matter how busy your day may be.

Prayer: *How often I fail to live what I teach. I confess to You, Father, that I need Your wisdom about how to live a godly life before my children (and anyone else* *who may see me as a role model). It has been said that how we live speaks much more loudly than the words we say, so help me to demonstrate the fruit of Your Spirit in all areas. Make me a joyful example to all those in my sphere of influence.*

Chapter Two

✷

Generously Give Giant Servings of Joy Juice

Have you had your Joy Juice today? Let's remember to cheerfully give some to others.

One of the best ways I know to be joyful is to have a grateful heart. Do you find yourself thanking God often for the many blessings of life? Or do you take much for granted? If we're not careful, we all fall into the trap of just expecting His provision and protection, taking it for granted. How often we fall short of thanking Him for all that He is and does for us. Our God is a giving God! Each of us benefits in countless ways from His generous nature. **Acts 14:17** says, *"He has shown kindness by giving you rain from heaven and crops in their seasons; he provides you with plenty of food and fills your hearts with joy."*

God delights in giving good gifts to His children. Remember **James 1:17**? *"Every good and perfect gift is from above."* So in order to express our thankfulness for His generosity, let's determine to be a *"cheerful giver"* (**2 Cor. 9:7**) and pass along the love of the Lord to others. Any time we give with a joyful attitude in the name of the Lord, whether its our money, our time, or our efforts, then we are bringing joy to our Father. He doesn't want us to give grudgingly, but cheerfully.

Ask God to show you where He would have you give back to Him. Then be obedient and generous as He leads you. Not only will you have peace and satisfaction, knowing that you have done as the Holy Spirit has lead you, but you will also experience that joy in the Lord that fills you up and makes you want to keep giving—for Him!

Prayer: *"Each of you should give what you have decided in your heart to give, not reluctantly or* *under compulsion, for God loves a cheerful giver"* **(2 Cor. 9:7).** *God, I admit that many times I don't give cheerfully, especially when it's of my time or tight resources. Show me ways to give of Your love so that my heart will grow more and more like Yours, filled with unconditional love, gratitude, and joy.*

Have you had your Joy Juice today? Give generously to your neighbors and friends so that your supply will continually multiply.

2 Corinthians 9: 6-8 is a clear explanation of why we should give generously:

Remember this: Whoever sows sparingly will also reap sparingly, and whoever sows generously will also reap generously. Each of you should give what you have decided in your heart to give, not reluctantly or under compulsion, for God loves a cheerful giver. And God is able to bless you abundantly,, so that in all things at all times, having all that you need, you will abound in every good work.

Paul was teaching that the reason we are to be cheerful in our giving is because God wants to bless us. If our heart attitude is right, we will give because we want to, *not* because we have to. When we feel obligated or compelled, there is no joy. But when we "*sow generously*" out of love for our Father, we will "*reap generously*." God promises that His grace will abound in our lives.

How can we do as the scripture says and be a cheerful giver? By giving away God's love and joy each day. Kneel before the Giver of all good things and seek His guidance. He will show you who, what, when, where, and how to share generously with others. Then, get ready for an extra serving of His Joy Juice!

Prayer: *Lord Jesus, tenderize my heart, and make me aware of ways I can give to others. Make me an ambassador for You, giving with Your love and Your kindness. Show me today ways that I can sow generously. Transform me into a cheerful giver so that I may share a double portion of Your joy with others.*

Have you had your Joy Juice today? Please share generously with others. Consider how you give of your resources as you read the following tale:

The story is told about a one dollar bill and a hundred dollar bill that got folded together and began talking about their life experiences. The hundred dollar bill began to brag: "I've had a great life," he said. "I've been to all the big hotels. Donald Trump himself used me at his casino. I've been in the wallets of Fortune 500 board members; I've flown from one end of the country to the other! I've even been in the wallet of two Presidents of the United States, and once when the Queen of England visited the US, she used me to buy a packet of gum."

In awe, the dollar humbly responded, "Gee, nothing like that has ever happened to me—but I have been to church a lot!" [1]

We smile at this rather humorous story, but there is some truth that rings through. Why is it that we are so willing to spend our money on things that don't last, but we hesitate to generously give to causes that further the Kingdom of God, causes which will last for an eternity?

In **Matthew 6:19-21,** Jesus warns his disciples:

Do not store up for yourselves treasures on earth, where moth and rust destroy, and where thieves break in and steal. But store up for yourselves treasures in heaven, where moth and vermin do not destroy, and where thieves do not break in and steal. For where your treasure is, there your heart will be also.

Where is your treasure? I hope it's your faith in God! Show your love for Him today by giving from your heart. As you do, get ready to experience true joy.

Prayer: *Stuff, lots of stuff. I confess that's what consumes a lot of my thoughts, my time, and my efforts. Lord, convict my heart of how unimportant the material possessions are. Renew in my heart a passion for sharing the Good News of you with others. I am beginning to realize that's how to have an abundance of joy in the Lord.*

Abundant Joy Juice

Have you had your Joy Juice today? Drink your fill, and then get ready to give some to others.

I have such sweet memories of an elderly gentleman that I had the privilege of knowing during my young adult years. He was different, but in a good sense of the word. He stood out from the crowd because He was always looking for ways that he could give to others. He would make things and give them away. He would cut flowers from his garden and deliver them to someone who needed a bright spot in his/her day. If he heard of a financial need, he would secretly take care of that need—without expecting anything in return.

One day I decided to do something to thank him for being so good to my family. I took him a gift and said, "Thank you for all you do for others." His response was humble as he said, "Oh, honey, don't you know, you can't ever give anything away. It always comes back to you multiplied!" Looking back now, I know that he had discovered the secret to having the joy of the Lord.

Let's take a lesson from this godly man. Look for opportunities to give. Don't worry about not having enough. When you share your joy and love, your energy and vitality, your time, money, and talents with other people, you don't lose anything. (It's all God's anyway.) In fact, sharing creates even more joy and love within you. And the people with whom you share often pass the giving spirit along to others. The more you share your blessings, the more blessings God showers on you, and the joyous cycle continues. We have this promise in **Luke 6:38:** *"Give, and it will be given to you."*

Prayer: *Thank You, God, for the countless blessings You shower on me every day. Give me a generous heart so that I will be always ready to share with others who You bring into my path. My desire is to share Your joy by giving, giving, giving. I know I can never out-give You, Father, but give me the desire to try.*

Abundant Joy Juice

Have you had your Joy Juice today? Are you drinking it cheerfully? If you've gotten into the habit of giving to others, you can count on a cheerful heart.

In the Bible, there is a direct link between generosity and cheerfulness. Remember the verses in **2 Corinthians 9:6, 7**:

Whoever sows sparingly will also reap sparingly, and whoever sows generously will also reap generously. Each of you should give what you have decided in your heart to give, not reluctantly or under compulsion, for God loves a cheerful giver.

Are you a cheerful giver? How much does a cheerful giver give? (Should I tell you that I just had the memory of the old tongue twister: "How much wood would a woodchuck chuck, if a woodchuck could chuck wood"? Okay, I won't tell you that!) Back to the question: how much does a cheerful giver give?

Many times we fear that we just won't have enough left for our own needs if we give too much. What we need to realize is that nothing we think we own is really ours. It all belongs to God. **Psalm 24:1** reminds us that *"the earth is the LORD's, and everything in it."* Whatever we consider ours is simply on loan from God. That's what stewardship is all about.

We are taught that we are to give God our tithe—10 percent of our income. But we cannot do this cheerfully until we understand that God gives us 100 percent to manage for Him. The tithe and offering is to test our hearts. Do we voluntarily and cheerfully give back to God? Does your heart pass the giving test?

Remember: you can't out-give God. Express your love for Him today by offering Him not only your tithe but also a joyful offering.

Prayer: *You are the Giver of all things, Lord. I praise You for that. Help me to see my material blessings as* *gifts on loan from You. Loosen my grip on them, and plant deep in my heart a desire to share with others. May the giving of my tithe and offerings become a sacrifice of joy. Make me a cheerful giver. I want to pass the giving test.*

Have you had your Joy Juice today? Drinking it faithfully helps you to see your blessings more clearly.

I've been thinking a lot lately about the word *blessing*. Maybe it's my season of life. I'm a "GiGi," you know...a grandmommy. As I think of how I love to favor my grandchildren, I am beginning to understand that God truly does enjoy blessing His children. For years I didn't think too much about the word *blessing*. It just meant a short, canned prayer that we said before each meal. It was a habit—a good habit—of words recited without much thought, just ritual and routine.

Often our prayer life does get stale and meaningless. We send up a "God is great; God is good. Let us thank Him for our food," yet we never stop to think about how truly blessed we are. May I challenge you (and you can challenge me, as well) to begin to be sensitive to the many blessings that are ours. To name a few:

- Good health
- Family

- Material comforts
- Our homes
- Good friends
- Freedom
- And most importantly, a God who loves us so much that He sent His Son to die for us.

My prayer for you today is the scripture found in **Numbers 6:24, 25:**

"May the LORD bless you and protect you. May the LORD smile on you and be gracious to you" (NLT).

Prayer: *Lord, I claim the above scripture as my prayer for my loved ones and for me personally today. I ask for Your blessing and protection. Please smile on us, and be gracious to us all. And give us thankful hearts for those blessings.*

Abundant Joy Juice

Have you had your Joy Juice today? Too busy? Well, bless your heart! Slow down and enjoy a serving before you get too stretched and stressed.

Our world is so fast paced that truly, many days, we miss out on the blessings that God wants to pour out on us. We hit the ground running and don't slow down long enough to give much thought to our relationship with God. Maybe we need to get up just a few minutes earlier each morning and simply *"be still"* before God (**Ps. 46:10**). To develop a personal relationship with Him, we must spend time in prayer and Bible study.

Read **Psalm 128:1, 2:** *"Blessed are all who fear the LORD, who walk in obedience to him. You will eat the fruit of your labor; blessings and prosperity will be yours."* This Psalm is sometimes called the marriage prayer because it was often sung at Israelite marriages. But we can all glean truth from studying this passage. God should be the true head of the home. He will reward our devotion to him with inner peace and blessings beyond measure. [2]

Abundant Joy Juice

The values outlined in God's Word include love, service, honesty, integrity, and prayer. If we don't take the time to read and study, then we're not going to know what these principles are or what the Bible teaches about them. We can't expect to experience pure, genuine joy in the Lord without digesting a steady spiritual diet of Bible study and prayer.

Now, slow down and sip your Joy Juice so that you'll be able to share the blessings of love and joy with others.

Prayer: *Dear Lord, I admit that many times I race through the day without ever slowing down long enough to hear from You. Draw me close to You and help me to walk in Your ways. Help me to prioritize my life in such a way that You are at the top of my list. Impress upon my heart how important it is that I spend time with You daily. Show me how to do that, and give me the desire and passion to make it happen.*

Have you had your Joy Juice today? You'll be blessed by drinking a huge serving and offering some to others as well.

God continues to pour out His blessings on us, doesn't He? But many times we miss them because we are so consumed with our problems or distractions. Often we're just so busy that we are simply oblivious to His goodness and graciousness. **Ephesians 1:3 says,** ***"Praise be to the God and Father of our Lord Jesus Christ, who has blessed us in the heavenly realms with every spiritual blessing in Christ."***

In Paul's letter to the Ephesians, he explains the wonderful things that we have received through Christ. He says that God has blessed us *"with every spiritual blessing in Christ."* Does this mean that we will never have tough times or problems? Not at all! But when we do go through the difficult times, we can face those challenges knowing that we have the blessing of God's strength, wisdom, and comfort—always.

If we choose to depend on Him, we have to look beyond Mt. Crisis and let Him carry us through to the other side. What's so scary is that we can't see what's on the other side of the mountain. We have to move forward in obedient faith. Many times God requires us to defy human logic and reason. He says, "Come, let me carry you to the top of this mountain. Just rest in my loving arms." **Matthew 11:28** proves his willingness to be our strength. Jesus said, *"Come to me, all you who are weary and burdened, and I will give you rest."*

Allow Jesus to carry your burdens, and watch Him pour out His blessings of love, compassion, and joy.

Prayer: *Many days I'm emotionally exhausted, Lord, and I simply don't know what to do. It's even hard to pray. Remind me that You are always there and want me to crawl up onto Your lap so that You can put Your arms of comfort around me. Physical* *rest is very important, too. I know that. But spiritual rest is what I most desire, and that rest can come only from You. Give me strength to lift my arms up to You and ask My Heavenly Father to pick me up and carry me, now and always.*

Abundant Joy Juice

Have you had your Joy Juice today? Turn on some good praise music as you drink a healthy serving of your juice. Praise and joy go together perfectly.

All through the Bible, we read about people lifting their voices in songs of praise to God. Sometimes our hearts are so full of excitement and gratefulness for the wonderful blessings the Lord has poured into our lives that it's easy to sing His praises. We feel like the psalmist of **Psalm 13:6** who wrote, *"I will sing the LORD's praise, for he has been good to me."*

But what about those times when we find ourselves in the valley of depression or despair? It's not nearly as easy to *"sing the LORD's praise"*, is it? That's when our faith should kick in, and instead of going with our feelings, we should make intentional choices to obey the Scripture and continue to believe that God is in control.

Rod Best explains it like this:

When we make a conscious decision to praise God no matter what, even though we may be going through a night season in our lives, God brings His Joy and His Peace and we enter into that rest which is ours as children of God. Sometimes heaviness of spirit will rob us of God's joy. We are to put on **the garment of praise for the spirit of heaviness** **(Isaiah 61:3)**.*³*

Wow! What a blessing to realize that our *"garment of praise"* is always the perfect accessory to our wardrobe of spiritual joy. Be sure to wear it everyday, and you will be blessed. Know that it's perfectly okay to share and let others wear your *"garment of praise"* if they are in need of a covering of joy.

Prayer: Psalm 89:1 *expresses my heart today, Lord: "I will sing of the LORD's great love forever; with my mouth I will make your faithfulness known through all generations." Whether I feel like praising or not, I will strive to make a conscious effort to praise You. Please don't let a spirit of heaviness rob me of Your joy.*

Have you had your Joy Juice today? Your faithful example will be a blessing to those who are looking to you as a role model.

Whatever stage of life you are in at the present, you are an influence on someone. If you are a parent or a grandparent (or a great-grandparent), your children are looking to you for an example. Many of you are brothers or sisters, aunts or uncles; all of us are friends of young people who may be modeling themselves after us — whether they even realize it or not.

We need to live each moment of every day with the mind-set that we should be a blessing to whoever is watching us. Need a little help in knowing how to do that? How do we bless these precious ones who are a part of our lives? Here are a few suggestions made by Claude Thomas, Pastor of First Baptist Church in Euless, Texas:

- *By praying for them. Let them know that they can depend on you to pray with them and for*

> *them. Pray for them, even when they don't seem to care if you are praying for them.*
> - *Encourage them. A pat on the back and an uplifting word can make such a difference in a person's attitudes and choices.*
> - *Explain to them that they are special and God has a wonderful plan for them.*
> - *Show them, by your own example, the joy of pursuing God's best in life.*
> - *Spend time with them, taking care to expose the truths of the Bible to them.* [4]

When we live out these very practical disciplines, we will discover the power of blessing—both in our own lives and in the lives of our children and all those who are looking for our guidance. Ask God's joyful blessing on these dear ones who look up to you as an example and role model.

Prayer: *Father, I am reminded of the old hymn, "Make Me a Channel of Blessing" by Harper G. Smith. May this be my prayer today:*

Make me a channel of blessing today,
Make me a channel of blessing, I pray;
My life possessing, my service blessing,
Make me a channel of blessing today. [5]

Have you had your Joy Juice today? See if you can catch someone in the act of drinking his/hers.

Since I retired from the educational arena, I've had the sweet privilege of volunteering at one of our local hospitals as Chaplain. Some of the patients are worried and anxious about their physical conditions. Others are excited young parents who have given birth to beautiful little bundles of joy.

There was one particular patient whom I had the privilege of meeting that left a lasting impression on me. I "caught" him in the act of being joyful, though most people would think he had no reason for expressing joy. Let's call him Danny. I want to share his story.

I knocked on Danny's hospital room door that day and was completely surprised by what I found when I pushed it open. There he lay, flat of his back in the bed, in prison garb, shackles on his feet, with two armed guards on each side of him. I glanced at my list to call him by name, took a deep breath, and uttered a silent prayer. "Lord, give me words, wisdom, and boldness." I greeted him with a smile. "Danny?"

"Danny G. from Tennessee!" he responded. I opened my mouth, and much to my surprise, I heard my own voice responding, "Well, I'm Joyce A. from the town of Wray!" We both had a laugh, and I immediately knew there was something special about this guy. He cheerfully invited me in and began to share with me about his physical condition, ending with these words: "I have cancer, and they give me about four months to live." The amazing thing was there was no sadness in his voice, not a trace.

"Do you know where you're going, Danny?" I asked. He responded confidently, "Oh, yes, Joyce A. from Wray! I'm going home." And he began to share of how the Lord had become a close, personal friend. He paused long enough to flash another smile, and then he asked me if he could "bless me." I didn't know what he had in mind, but I shook my head in agreement. He began to recite (with such passion, love, and joy) the most beautiful poem I'd ever heard about Jesus dying on the cross.

By the time he had finished, a river of tears was streaming down my cheeks. There was not a dry eye in the room. Danny had shown me (and those big, burly prison guards) what the scripture in **Philippians 4:4** means when it says, *"Rejoice in the Lord always."*

I had the privilege of praying with my brother Danny that day. As I turned to leave I said, "Danny, indeed, I have been blessed by meeting to you." With tears glistening in his eyes and a serene smile upon his face he humbly responded, "I just hope you've seen a glimpse of Jesus today."

I don't know what Danny did in his past to be a federal prisoner, but I discovered that day that it truly didn't matter. What I do know is that he was forgiven, and he will spend eternity with Christ. That assurance is why he was overflowing with joy. Are you sure of your salvation? I earnestly beg you to take care of that today and be assured of a joyful eternity with Christ—and Danny.

Prayer: *Father, I know that I'm a sinner. I confess my sins before you and accept you into my life as my Savior and Lord. Thank you for saving me. Now, help me to break free from the prison and bondage to sin as I allow you to be in control of my life.*

Abundant Joy Juice

Have you had your Joy Juice today? Drink up, and see if anyone catches you being joyful.

People do notice when you are a consistent model of joy. That's a promise! All of us are joyful from time to time; it's the "consistent" part that's not always easy. Is it your heart's desire to be a joyful example before others? Then here are some joy tips:

- First, we must accept Christ as our personal Savior and Lord and consistently live for Him.
- We should be faithful to study the Bible and to apply God's commands and instructions to our daily lives.
- We need an active and steady prayer life.
- We should never base our faith on our feelings. We should be intentional and unfailing about practicing the joy of the Lord, regardless of what's going on in our lives.

Let me tell you about a friend that I've consistently caught being reliably joyful. She is a role model for many when it comes to being a joyful Christian. I've seen her go through times of sickness and the death of a parent; she is now caring for an aging, ailing husband. Nevertheless, she always gives God the glory for carrying her through these circumstances. She continually and consistently expresses joy in and through her relationship with God.

This dear lady studies the Word daily and has for years. It's hidden in her heart. Her life exemplifies the scripture found in **Proverbs 3:5** that says, *"Trust in the LORD with all your heart and lean not on your own understanding."*

That trust is the secret to having genuine joy. Joy is not found in complaining about our uncomfortable situations. Rather, joy follows when we trust that God has us in His hands and in His plans.

Let others catch you drinking your Joy Juice consistently. Choose to share His joy with others—twenty-four hours a day, seven days a week, week after week, month after month, and year after year.

Just think, that kind of consistency will lead to a joyful eternity with Jesus!

Prayer: *May I live each day faithfully for You, Lord. May I be a solid example of joy to all those around me. Even when I don't understand why certain things are happening, help me steadily to trust You. Thank you for being my Savior, my Lord, my comforter, my counselor. Use me, Father, to further Your kingdom, and may You receive all glory and honor as I consistently serve You.*

Chapter Three

✳

**Abundant Helpings
Of
Joy Juice**

Have you had your Joy Juice today? Feel free to take an abundant helping for yourself.

Doesn't the verse in **John 10:10** bring a smile to your face? Jesus said, ***"I am come that they might have life, and that they might have it more abundantly"*** **(KJV)**.

What an awesome, humbling truth! Jesus came to this earth to live and die for you and me that we may enjoy abundant life. That's a life filled with joy, people! He doesn't want us simply to survive. He wants us to *thrive*.

It's a sad thing that many people think abundance is simply about accumulating possessions—a big house, an expensive automobile, and/or lots of money. The abundance Jesus is talking about goes far beyond material things. It means being content with what God has given us and expressing gratitude and joy *even* during tough times. Some of the most joyful people you will ever meet are those who have a close relationship with the Lord. It has nothing to do with how rich or poor they are by the world's standards.

Are you living in God's abundance? We can profess to be a Christian and miss out on the abundant life because we are not 100 percent committed to Him. Ask God to take over every part of your life. That's how to experience the abundant life, overflowing with joy.

Prayer: *Thank you, thank you, thank you, Father, for all You have given me. I am rich in relationship with You, regardless of what my bank account may be today. Your daily love deposits in my spiritual bank fill my heart with joy, and there is nothing more satisfying than to be filled up with joy in the Lord. Give me an insatiable appetite for an abundant life in You.*

Have you had your Joy Juice today? Drinking it faithfully is so important to assure abundant joy.

Abundance—what does that word mean to you? When I see or hear the word, I immediately think of a huge amount of something. Sometimes we think we have an abundance of work. Many days moms have an abundance of laundry and housework. Dads probably feel that they have an abundance of yard work and chores. Most likely, we all feel that we have an abundance of bills.

But let's think of abundance in the manner that Jesus taught about in John. Remember **John 10:10**, the passage we talked about in the previous devotional? **It says, *"I have come that they may have life, and have it to the full."*** What kind of abundance is Jesus speaking of in this verse?

In *The Prayer of Jabez*, Bruce Wilkinson tells us that the secret to true abundance is to want what God wants. That means that we love God so much that we put aside our desires and trust that God knows what is best for us. He wants us to bring our needs and desires before Him, but when we do so, we need to be content with whatever answer He gives us. [1]

Abundant life in Christ is living every moment soaking up His love, His will, and His direction. It is then that we will be filled with abundant joy.

Prayer: *Abundant joy, that's my prayer today. I desire abundant joy that comes from loving You supremely. Help me to want what You want for me and be satisfied with the answers to my prayers. I trust You to know what is best for me, Lord. Open my heart and pour a double portion of Your love and joy down deep into my soul until it spills out and overflows onto others.*

Abundant Joy Juice

Have you had your Joy Juice today? Drink it abundantly!

If you are one of the joyful Christians who has asked Jesus in your heart, be ready to share the good news with others. When folks ask why you are so joyful, tell them that they, too, can find their own personal servings of Joy Juice by going to the storehouse of God's Word. Show them in Scripture how to have a relationship with Christ. That's where the Joy Juice of Jesus is stored for anyone who seeks.

Some people find it difficult to tell others about how to have a personal relationship with Jesus. It's really as simple as A, B, C. The steps are easy to remember:

A: Admit that you are a sinner: ***"For all have sinned and fall short of the glory of God"*** **(Rom. 3:23).**

B: Believe that Jesus died for you: ***"But God demonstrates his own love for us in this:***

> *While we were still sinners, Christ died for us"* **(Rom. 5:8).**

C: Confess your sins: *"That if you confess with your mouth, 'Jesus is Lord,' and believe in your heart that God raised him from the dead, you will be saved"* **(Rom. 10:9).**[2]

A, B, C—Admit, Believe, Confess. It's that simple. Lead someone to Christ today, and experience a double portion of abundant joy.

Prayer: *What a privilege it is to share Your Good News, Jesus! Make me aware of any divine appointment that You have set up for me today. Fill me with boldness to win someone to Christ. It's as easy as A, B, C, right? So why do I feel so hesitant, so nervous? Am I ashamed of my relationship with You? No! Then give me the words, and open the right doors. I'm ready—if You will go with me.*

Have you had your Joy Juice today? God always has an abundant supply ready to give away to those who ask.

When you pray, do you ask God to bless you abundantly? Or do you think that would be selfish? Through the years, I've discovered that our Heavenly Father *delights* in our coming before Him and asking Him to pour out His blessings on us.

Just think about it like this. If you are a parent (or grandparent) and one of your children comes to you humbly with open hands, what is your first question? Probably something like, "What do you need, sweetheart?" If they respond by telling you their desire but also express that they want you to give them what you think is best, won't you be touched?

Is that our attitude when we go to our Heavenly Father? Or do we give Him our Christmas wish list? The next time you ask God for something, examine your request, and see if you can truly say, "God, this is my desire, but I trust that You know what is best for me." If we would start praying like this, we might be astonished at all the blessings that would begin to flow.

Philippians 3:8 is a great life verse: *"I consider everything a loss because of the surpassing worth of knowing Christ Jesus my Lord."* Paul had discovered the secret to abundance: a genuine, bold, joyful love for the Lord.

Have you discovered that secret for yourself?

Prayer: *"Oh, Lord, that You would bless me, indeed"* **(1 Chron. 4:10, NASB).** *That's how Jabez prayed, and today I am following the example of his prayer. Bless me abundantly with love for You. Pour out Your Joy Juice into my life so that I may overflow onto and into others' lives. I want to be a vessel for You, bursting forth with Your goodness, mercy, love, and abundant joy.*

Abundant Joy Juice

Have you had your Joy Juice today? God wants to drench you from head to toe with His abundant love and joy.

From an early age, we're taught about keeping score. In sporting events, the way to tell who wins the game is to keep score. In business, legers have to be kept so that the company can be run efficiently and effectively. In families, a list is sometimes made in order to keep track of chores. And in many relationships, people keep score of all the negatives.

Because of these experiences with keeping score, we sometimes have a skewed mindset of how God keeps track of whose turn it is to receive a blessing. Thank goodness, God does *not* work the same way we do. He doesn't have a bookkeeper angel who says, "Wait, God! You already blessed him three times this week." Or, "Pardon me, God, but don't you think you're over-blessing her?"

God doesn't set a quota for His goodness and blessing. We must never hesitate to go to our loving Father and present our requests to Him. I'm not

Abundant Joy Juice

---

talking about selfish requests, but prayers which indicate that we desire His best for us. (Just keep in mind that His best might not be a six-figure income or a vacation in paradise!) If our heart is in tune with His heart, then we will ask for blessings according to His will.

Look at this verse in **Malachi 3:10**:

'And try Me now in this,' says the LORD of hosts, 'If I will not open for you the windows of heaven, And pour out for you such blessing that there will not be room enough to receive it.' **(KJV)**

Pull out your umbrella, put on your raincoat, and slide into those joy boots. Get ready to be drenched with a downpour of blessings of joy.

Prayer: My prayer today is in the form of the song "Showers of Blessing" by Daniel W. Whittle.

Abundant Joy Juice

There shall be showers of blessing:
This is the promise of love;
There shall be seasons refreshing,
Sent from the Savior above.
Showers of blessing,
Showers of blessing we need:
Mercy drops round us are falling,
But for the showers we plead.
There shall be showers of blessing,
Precious reviving again;
Over the hills and the valleys,
Sound of abundance of rain.
There shall be showers of blessing;
Send them upon us, O Lord;
Grant to us now a refreshing,
Come, and now honor Thy Word.
There shall be showers of blessing:
Oh, that today they might fall,
Now as to God we're confessing,
Now as on Jesus we call!
There shall be showers of blessing,

If we but trust and obey;
There shall be seasons refreshing,
If we let God have His way.
Showers of blessing,
Showers of blessing we need:
Mercy drops round us are falling,
But for the showers we plead. [3]

Have you had your Joy Juice today? Let me encourage you to drink it faithfully.

One of the most glowing characteristics a person can possess is the gift of encouragement. Some people seem to have been born with the ability to edify and build others up. Others, I believe, have developed the skill through the years. But those who are most natural with sharing encouragement seem to be the ones who have the God-given gift of exhortation.

What does it mean to have "the gift" of exhortation? In the New Testament, encouragement and exhortation are often used to translate the same Greek word. A person who has the gift of encouragement will most often:

- Recognize someone's need and respond to that need in a caring and appropriate manner.
- Know what a person needs to hear and will say it in a timely fashion.
- Provide encouragement in a unique way that fits his/her own personality and experience.

Abundant Joy Juice

- Have lots of friends, because people love to be around them. After all, *everyone* needs encouragement.

Romans 12 tells about the different gifts given to believers. In this passage, Paul teaches us that if we have been given the gift of encouragement, then we should encourage. Please find someone who needs your encouragement today. You both will experience joy—the encouraging joy of the Lord.

Prayer: *Father, I want to be an encourager. Even if I don't have the natural gift of exhortation, I am asking for the grace to practice encouragement every day. Help me to read facial expressions and body language; give me insight into certain situations which can be helped by speaking a timely word or giving a little hug. Let others see You in me, and may I share with them the abundant joy that can be theirs by allowing You to have first place in their lives.*

Abundant Joy Juice

Have you had your Joy Juice today? Please encourage others to have their own personal serving.

It's easy for some people to encourage others because they have the gift of exhortation, given to them by the Divine Encourager. However, all of us are not born with the natural inclination toward being an encourager. Some of us truly are *not* gifted in this area. Nevertheless, our natural inclinations don't excuse us from trying to learn to encourage others.

The Word of God is filled with examples of encouragers, and we are shown how many were blessed by their encouragement. One example is Joseph. He learned the need for encouragement. He was not a natural encourager and didn't become one until God disciplined him into becoming one. We see an example of his encouragement in **Genesis 49**; he not only forgave his brothers, but he encouraged them. Joseph ended up being an encouragement to the whole people of Israel. We can't use the excuse that "we weren't born with the personality" to encourage people. The Bible instructs us to be encouragers—and that settles it.

Sometimes God might call us to be an encouragement to someone by helping them fulfill God's purpose in their life. Remember Aaron and Hur in **Exodus 17**? They held up Moses' arms during battle. This story reminds us that sometimes God calls us to lift others up, to help them accomplish a specific task for which God has anointed them.

Who does God want you to lift up today? Be willing and available to be used by God to share His encouragement and joy with others.

Prayer: *Dear Lord, I know how good it feels to be encouraged. Bring to my remembrance that feeling each time I find myself debating whether to enter in and be an encouragement to someone or whether just to stay safely un-entangled. I am always uplifted when someone shares a word of exhortation with me, so may I pay it forward and lift up someone today by sharing the joy of the Lord and a word of encouragement.*

Abundant Joy Juice

Have you had your Joy Juice today? Yes? Good job! I'm so proud of you!

An important part of encouragement is something called *affirmation*. It's not a difficult concept. It's simply letting someone know that you believe in them or that you're proud of them; it's a pat on the back, so to speak. Genuine words of affirmation can change a person's life—literally.

We've all heard stories of how teachers have made a difference in the lives of their students. And this is so true. But I want to come at this concept from a different perspective today. You see, I was a teacher for many years, and I want to give credit where credit is due. Time and time again it was the *children* who were an encouragement to me.

Unconditional, unsolicited hugs were mine each day from my primary and elementary school students. The smiles they so freely shared perked me up on even the toughest of days. Many times, I'd receive an original piece of artwork with an "I love you" scribbled across the page. Not only did these offerings fill my heart with joy, but it gave me affirmation that I was right where God meant for me to be.

I believe that we adults should take lessons from our younger friends. Reach out to that someone who needs a hug today. Generously share your smiles. Whether you know a person or not, it's a fact that everyone needs a smile. If nothing else, it affirms that the person is important enough to be acknowledged.

Share your talents with others who may need just the kind of "pick me up" that only you can give. When you get into the habit of being an encourager, then the joy of the Lord pours out *from* you and flows back *to* you. That's what you call "abundant joy."

Prayer: *My precious Father, God. I come to You today with a child-like heart, a child-like love, and a child-like faith, believing that You are the true Source of encouragement and all things good. When I see someone today who needs building up, help me to open my mouth and let You speak through me. If there* *is one who is sad or discouraged, open my arms, and let Your love wrap around them. If there is a personal need, give me Your discernment to detect that need, and then give me Your wisdom to know how to meet it. May I overflow with abundant joy onto many people in need today and tomorrow and the next day.*

Abundant Joy Juice

Have you had your Joy Juice today? Drink a few extra ounces if you are in need of encouragement.

Some mornings we need extra encouragement, don't we? Maybe we're dreading an appointment, or maybe we have such a busy day planned that we don't know how we're going to get it all done. It might be that we are suffering due to the loss of a loved one through death or a broken relationship. Many days we wake up tired and just don't have the energy to face the day cheerfully. How do we make it through days like that, days when we are feeling *dis*couraged?

We need to do as David did in **1 Samuel 30:6**: ***"But David strengthened himself in the LORD his God."*** Did you read that? He ***strengthened himself.*** Can we strengthen and encourage ourselves? Yes, we can! (Pardon me, I do not mean to steal anyone's campaign slogan.) How can we accomplish this?

- First of all, we have to get our heads on straight and start thinking about all our blessings instead of dwelling on all the perceived negatives in our life.

- Go back to very basic reasons for encouragement. Remember that if we have accepted Jesus into our life, He has promised never to leave us or forsake us.
- Read the scripture every day. This consistency is especially important when we feel discouraged. You'll be surprised at how many verses you'll find in which God speaks words of encouragement to your heart.
- Stop listening to and repeating the lies of the enemy; instead, concentrate on the promises of God.
- Meditate on His goodness.
- Pray about everything.

When you do these things, you'll be *"strengthen[ing] [your]self in the LORD."* Don't wait for someone else to come along with the solution to your discouragement. Determine to be joyful *now*.

Prayer: *Some days are tougher than others, Lord. Of course, You know that. Thank you that I can always call on You, no matter whether it's a good day or a bad day. Help me to refrain from throwing myself pity parties and focusing on all that's wrong. Instead, draw me closer and closer to You so that I will be resting in Your strength and wisdom. That's where my encouragement comes from—YOU. And that assurance brings me joy!*

Abundant Joy Juice

Have you had your Joy Juice today? Please encourage those around you to drink it faithfully.

Why do we need to be encouragers to those around us? I can think of several reasons right off the top of my head:

- It builds them up and makes then realize they have self-worth.
- It demonstrates a caring attitude.
- When you encourage them, you are displaying a Christian role model.
- Everyone needs an encouraging word.
- The world would be a much better place if we all determined to be encouragers.

But the main reason I believe we should want to be an encourager is simply because the Bible says so. Just as the song says, "Jesus loves me this I know, for the Bible tells me so," the Bible also tells us to encourage each other. Time and time again, we find verses such as the following:

Therefore encourage (admonish, exhort) one another and edify (strengthen and build up) one another, just as you are doing. **(1 Thess. 5:11, AMP)**

But encourage one another daily, as long as it is called 'Today,' so that none of you may be hardened by sin's deceitfulness. **(Heb. 3:13)**

In these verses and many other times throughout the Word of God, we are instructed to encourage. Are you being obedient? You'll be surprised at how much joy you'll share and how encouraged you will be when you become God's encouraging mouthpiece.

Prayer: *May I be an encouragement to someone today. Show me who needs that extra smile, word, or touch, Lord, and lead me to know how to build them up. Help me to realize what a great opportunity that will be to share Your love and joy with others.*

Abundant Joy Juice

Have you had your Joy Juice today? If you are drinking it on the go, be careful to watch your step so that you won't fall.

Proverbs is a power-packed book of wisdom. Each time I read it, I gain more insight into why God gives us certain commands and instructions. It's for our good! He does not want us to fall, spiritually. He loves us and wants to protect us. What's sad is that often we think we know better, and we run straight toward trouble, simply by not allowing God to be our top priority.

Look at **Proverbs 28:14:** *"Blessed is the one who always trembles before God, but whoever hardens their heart falls into trouble."* In this verse *tremble* means to revere and honor God. It has to do with respecting Who He is. We are to make sure that our heart stays tender toward him. We don't ever want to get to a place spiritually in which our hearts are hardened.

Have you learned to recognize God's voice when He speaks to you? Do you bring before Him every decision, regardless of how major or minor it may seem? Can you *"rejoice in the Lord always"* (**Phil. 4:4**)? If so, that's wonderful. That's a sure sign that your heart is tender toward Him. However, if you are not able to answer yes to all of these questions, maybe you need to stop and assess whether you have allowed your heart to become hardened. Remember what our verse for today says: *"whoever hardens their heart falls into trouble."* Trouble and callousness toward God are opposite to the abundant life we all desire.

Please listen to God as He leads you today. When you are in tune with His will, abundant joy will be yours.

Prayer: *How many times I've stumbled; how many times I've fallen flat on my face. But You, Father, are always there to pick me up. I do not want to fall because of a hardened heart. Guard my heart, Lord.*

Keep my heart tender and my eyes and ears tuned toward Your voice and Your plan. I'm striving toward an abundant life in You. Hold my hand, Lord, so that I will not fall.

Have you had your Joy Juice today? I've discovered that it tastes abundantly better when you share it with someone.

Isn't it wonderful to have good friends? They are God's joyful blessings to help us through tough times and celebrate with us in the good times. Listen to what the Bible has to say in **Ecclesiastes 4:9, 10**: *"Two are better than one, because they have good return for their labor: If either of them falls down, one can help the other up. But pity anyone who falls and has no one to help them up."*

These verses emphasize how we need one another; two are better than one. Do you surround yourself with friends, or do you prefer to do everything by yourself? Oh, people! Please include your friends in your daily life. You miss out on so much when you don't.

Friends provide support, laughter, encouragement, and companionship. They are there to share your tears, pick you up when you're down, and pray for you anytime. But the key to having friends is that you must first be one yourself. Make the effort to reach out to people; don't wait for them to come to you. Show yourself friendly as **Proverbs 18:24** teaches **(KJV)**. When you do, you will find the blessing of friendship to be one of your greatest pleasures.

Good friends are treasures who will be there when you fall, encouraging you to get up and go on. Christian friends are an important part of the abundant life in Christ. Just remember that your best friend should always be Jesus. Thank Him for the gift of friendship as you pray specifically for your wonderful friends today. I'll just bet your heart will be overflowing with joy when your prayer of thanksgiving is complete.

Prayer: *Today I want to mention some of my best friends by name. God, I thank you for _____ and what he/she means to me. Thank You that we can hold each other* *accountable and encourage one another to walk more closely with You. Thank You for our times of laughter and the times we've shed tears together. That's what friends are for—to stick close through all circumstances. May I be a better friend as I grow in my relationship with You.*

Chapter Four

�֍

Children
Love
Joy Juice

Have you had your Joy Juice today? Children love the taste. Please share some with them every chance you get.

As I write this devotional, my family members are anxiously awaiting the arrival of two new grandbabies. Our two sons are blessing us with babies whose due dates are five days apart. (Of course, their precious wives will be doing the actual *work*.) We don't know yet whether we've got girls or boys or one of each, but what we do know is that they will be joyful blessings in our lives—no matter what. From the time we first learned of the pregnancies, we have been praying for these little ones. We have asked God's blessing on their lives.

How important it is to pray! We should make it a daily habit to pray for our children, grandchildren, young friends, and relatives. Many times I think we miss the importance of covering our young people in prayer. Raising small children is no easy task. It's a full time job with little time for rest. Parents seldom receive appreciation for the constant assignment of child-rearing, yet it is the most rewarding job on earth.

If you find yourself in this season of life, know that you can depend on God to give you wisdom when you need it most. Ask Him to fill your heart with love and compassion and forgiveness, to place on your tongue words of encouragement and edification. Some tasks may have to go undone. I can promise you that your children will not remember the dust on the furniture, but they will remember you holding them and reading them Bible stories. They will remember the sound of your voice as you pray with them and for them. They'll remember the songs you sing together about Jesus and His love.

Proverbs 22:6 tells us to *"Train up a child in the way he should go: and when he is old, he will not depart from it" (KJV).* Remember, you are making memories for your children. Make sure that they are memories filled with abundant joy.

Prayer: *Father, today I first want to thank You for the children You have put in my life. I give You praise for their special qualities and uniqueness. Thank You for allowing me to help mold them into joyful little persons who will grow up to love and serve You. May I always be a godly example of Your love and joy. Show me opportunities to guide them today.*

Abundant Joy Juice

Have you had your Joy Juice today? Keep your pantry well stocked so that you'll always have plenty for your family.

Many of you who are reading this devotional are parents or grandparents. Do you realize that no one else can pray for your little ones like you can? The genuine love you have for your children, the tenderness you feel for them, and your knowledge of their personality, needs, and challenges qualifies you to plead with God on their behalf with an urgency and earnestness which cannot be matched. When God speaks of his willingness to hear our prayers, He's coming from the standpoint of His parental love. Ponder the scripture in **Luke 11:13**. Jesus said, *"If you then, though you are evil, know how to give good gifts to your children, how much more will your heavenly Father give the Holy Spirit to those who ask him!"*

Our children are surrounded by evil influences—nobody denies that. This culture makes our role in praying for their protection even more imperative.

Abundant Joy Juice

Our God is a powerful, loving God, and He listens to our prayers on behalf of our children. We should pray without ceasing. Pray about everything: their decisions, their friends, their health, their spiritual condition. Most importantly, we should set a consistent, godly example before them. In the words of one wise man, *"Who you are speaks louder to me than anything you can say."* [1]

Is your life "speaking" the joy of Jesus? It's even okay to shout!

Prayer: *Jesus, I know You love the little children. Give me Your love so that I can share it with all the little ones You bring into my path today. I earnestly and fervently pray for my special loved ones who need Your touch— physically, emotionally, spiritually, or however. I ask for insight into their hearts and lives so that I can help them as You see fit. Lead me as I try to lead them.*

Abundant Joy Juice

Have you had your Joy Juice today? As you sip your juice this day, don't forget to pray for the children.

In the two previous devotionals, we've discussed the importance of praying for our children and setting a consistent, godly example before them. We can't expect them to do what we say if we're not modeling it ourselves. As parents, we want to be honored by our children. But we must live our lives in such a way that they want to give us honor.

In Adrian Roger's book *Ten Secrets for a Successful Family*, he suggests that one of the most important things we can do to gain our children's honor is to simply *love them*. Real parental love is not giving our children everything they want, but it is giving them what they need. [2]

How do we show our love? We can express it in a variety of ways. One way to love our children is simply by touching them. Nothing indicates our love any better than a hug, a pat on the back, or simply holding a hand. We also can show our children love by blessing them. *"The tongue has the power of life and death"* as **Proverbs 18:21** reminds us. So speak blessings over their lives; let them hear you say the words of blessing aloud.

Another expression of love for your children is listening to them. If we are too busy to listen, then they will soon stop trying to talk with us because they'll believe that we think something else is more important. Always be willing to spend time listening to your child.

These are just a few suggestions to gain honor from your children. Remember, with honor comes a heart full of joy.

Prayer: *Show me, Father, the children who need that special touch today. When I reach out, may Your love radiate through my touch and my words. Guard my tongue, especially when I get irritated and agitated. Fill me with Your patience and kindness so that I'm* *willing to take the time to listen when one needs to talk. May I never demand honor, but may I deserve it because I am following in Your footsteps.*

(Much of the information in today's devotional comes from Adrian Rogers' *Ten Secrets for a Successful Family*.)

Abundant Joy Juice

Have you had your Joy Juice today? I pray that you have because—whether you know it or not—someone is watching your example.

Are you in the habit of praying? I'm not just talking about saying the rote blessing before meals or the "Now I lay me down to sleep" when we go to bed at night. I'm talking about real, heart-felt communication with God.

Even the youngest child understands that prayer means talking to God. But they won't know *how* to pray until they see it and hear it modeled before them. It is never too soon to pray with and for your children.

As parents hold their infant, they can pray for his/her growth and development, for his love for the Lord, for wisdom, and for protection. As the child grows, if he hears his dad or mom praying, he will learn to emulate those prayers. Before long, the child will be praying from his heart. What a sweet, joyful sound, to hear a young one praying. If a child learns to pray when he is young, he is much more likely to continue to pray when he's a teenager and an adult.

God loves to hear all of our prayers, because we are all his children. I'm almost certain, however, that the innocent, sincere prayers of a child must touch His heart in a special way. Encourage your children in their prayer lives by helping them to memorize scriptures to pray. For example: "Help me, Father, to ***rejoice in the Lord always. I will say it again: REJOICE!"*** **(Phil. 4:4).**

Prayer: *Heavenly Father, help me to be aware that little ones are watching my example. Give me wisdom and boldness to pray aloud with them so that they can learn how to pray. Help me to display before them a sincere, transparent faith that places You first in all things and demonstrates that we are not ashamed to proclaim You as Lord.*

Abundant Joy Juice

Have you had your Joy Juice today? With every gulp, send up a prayer for a child.

If you are in love with a child, you will readily admit how special children are. They are gifts from God. We should be striving to be a good role model for them. We agree that it's so important to pray for them and with them—as well as teaching them to pray from their hearts.

One of the most rewarding things about raising children is to witness them grow into young adults who love the Lord and live according to His Word. That's not to say that they won't make mistakes along the way; many times, that's the way they learn. We must admit that their parents (and grandparents) aren't perfect either. That's why it is of utmost importance that we all depend on God to lead us and direct our paths.

When we first give birth to our children, it's hard to imagine that they will ever become adults, yet that time comes all too quickly. Our role as parent changes when they become adult children. We've spent 18 or so years investing in them and striving to teach them how to think on their own. We must realize that we no longer need to give our advice unless it's asked for. That's really difficult for some of us.

One thing will forever remain constant: our children will *always* need our prayers. Regardless of age, stage of life, or circumstances, we should continue to cover them in prayer. My sweet eighty-something year old mother continues to pray for me, my siblings, all her grandchildren, and her great-grandchildren. We all desire her prayers because we know God listens joyfully to His special friend.

Do the same for all the children in your life. And leave them a joyfully prayerful legacy.

Prayer: *Today, dear Lord, I am praying for all the children that You have entrusted to my care. Bring them to my mind all through the day so that I will continually lift them before Your throne.*

Abundant Joy Juice

Have you had your Joy Juice today? It'll remind you how very special you are to the Lord.

When I was working in the primary and elementary school setting, I would often teach a lesson about how unique and special each of us are. I'd have the children look at their fingerprints and remind them that no two people—not even twins—have the same set of fingerprints. Each one is different and unique.

Sometimes we'd do an art project in which they would put their thumbs in paint or ink and make a picture using their thumbprints. I'd summarize the lesson by telling them they were "thumbbody special." (I learned this concept many years ago from Mamie McCullough, professional speaker and author.) [3]

The children and I decided that we'd have a secret signal to speak to one another in the hallways or whenever we were supposed to be quiet in other areas of the school building. We'd give one another a "thumbs up." That not only meant "Hello," but it was also a way to let that other person know that we thought they were "thumbbody special." It blesses my heart that I often meet some of my former students, who are adults now, and they lift that thumb and smile. Some even verbalize, "You are thumb-body special!" That truly warms my heart and gives me a feeling of being loved.

Do you know how special you are, especially to God? In **Matthew 10:30** Jesus tells us that *"even the very hairs of your head are all numbered."* You are so valuable to Him that He knows every detail about you. He demonstrated that love by sending His only Son to die for you. That should fill each of our hearts with great joy.

Prayer: *Father, give me a child-like faith. Help me to see my uniqueness and be thankful for how You made me. Reveal to me Your purpose in my life by using the talents, abilities, and gifts that you have given specifically to me. Though I am no **more** important than anyone else, I am "thumbbody special" because You created me. Help me to always remember that as I share that joy with others today.*

Have you had your Joy Juice today? Drinking it daily reminds you how dearly loved you are by God.

Most people don't realize their importance in God's eyes. They just see themselves as one of billions who are in this vast world. They believe that God could not possibly think they're special. He is much too busy to be bothered by their concerns.

How far from the truth! You see, God is God. He can listen to each of us simultaneously as we bring our needs before Him. He doesn't play favorites because He loves us all. In other words, *you* are special to God!

Listen to Jesus' prayer to our Father in **John 17:23.** Jesus prayed the following: ***"I in them and you in me—so that they may be brought to complete unity. Then the world will know that you sent me and have loved them even as you have loved me."***

Did you hear Jesus say that God loves you? That's why He sent Jesus—to live and die for you.

One woman expressed her understanding of that truth like this:

I can't get round it; I can't burrow under it or climb over it. So the only thing I can do is go through it, absorbing it as I go. Christ is in me—and God loves me as much as he loves Christ. And no way can God's love for Christ be half-hearted. I went to sleep snuggling into that verse last night. [4]

May you and I snuggle into that truth, as well. Not only as we fall asleep tonight, but also as we face each challenge of the day. May the knowledge of God's love bring you much joy.

Prayer: *Dear Lord, it is incomprehensible how much You love me. I am unworthy of Your love, yet You still sent Your Son to die for me. Only the Divine Father could love like that. I am so thankful for Your love, Your faithfulness, Your plan for my life. It fills my heart with great joy.*

Abundant Joy Juice

Have you had your Joy Juice today? It'll make you shine with joy!

Don't you love to hear the voices of little children singing? They don't care if they are on key or not. They sing because they enjoy it. And have you noticed that when they forget the words, they can just make up their own?

Let's revisit some of the songs that we used to sing as children. Maybe you've taught them to your children or grandchildren. Most of these choruses will be familiar to you. As we look at the words again with fresh eyes, let's see if we can squeeze new joy from the lyrics.

Do you remember the children's song "This Little Light of Mine" by Dixon Loes (written about 1920)?

This little light of mine,
I'm gonna let it shine.
This little light of mine,
I'm gonna let it shine.
This little light of mine,

I'm gonna let it shine.
Let it shine,
Let it shine,
Let it shine.

Then it continues with verses that say:
Hide it under a bushel? NO!
I'm gonna let it shine.

Won't let Satan blow it out,
I'm gonna let it shine.

Let it shine til Jesus comes,
I'm gonna let it shine. [5]

Catchy little tune, isn't it? I can hear some of you singing right now. As you sing, please consider what it really means to let your light shine. **Matthew 5:16** commands us to *"**Let your light shine before others, that they may see your good deeds and glorify your Father in heaven.**"* When we put God first in our lives, we will have a joy in our heart that illuminates our life. We'll shine with His love for others. We'll be bright ambassadors for Him. Our purpose will be to glorify Him in all that we do and say. So, let your light shine with joy.

Prayer: *Lord Jesus, may I be a "light" in this dark world. When others see me and the life I am living, please help me to shine with Your love, Your joy, Your compassion. Open my heart and empty me of* **me**. *Fill me up with* **You***; that's the only way I can always shine with the joy of Jesus.*

Have you had your Joy Juice today? Jesus loves for you to drink it faithfully. Let the words of this childhood song penetrate your heart today:

Jesus loves me! This I know,
For the Bible tells me so.
Little ones to Him belong;
They are weak, but He is strong.
Yes, Jesus, loves me!
Yes, Jesus loves me!
Yes, Jesus loves me!
The Bible tells me so. [6]

In years past, most every child in this country could sing the words to this song. It was one of the favorites to sing in and out of Sunday School or Vacation Bible School and at other gatherings, formal and informal. But the sad truth these days is that many of our children have never heard this precious song; many adults, who once sung it as children, have forgotten the truth of its words.

Jesus loves you and me. The only proof that we need that this love is true is stated in the song: "*the Bible tells me so.*" If it's in the Bible, it is truth; for every word is God-breathed. He inspired each Old Testament and New Testament writer to pen His thoughts. (It's not some make-believe story, nor is it a collection of folk tales or fables.) From Genesis to Revelation, every word is from God. He tells us over and over again that we are loved.

One verse reads as follows:

Jesus loves me still today,
Walking with me on my way,
Wanting as a friend to give
Light and love to all who live. [6]

No matter which verses you choose to sing, there will always be truth and joy in the fact that Jesus loves us; yes, each and every one of us is loved.

Prayer: *Jesus, thank you for loving me! Put this tune in my mind and the song in my heart so that I may sing it throughout this day. Help me to focus on the words and the truth that they speak to me, personally. The Bible tells of Your love and Your strength when I am weak. May I be a reflection of Your love to others today.*

Have you had your Joy Juice today? Let it soak *deep* into your heart and be reminded of how *wide* is the love of our Lord.

Do you remember singing the beloved children's song "Deep and Wide"? It was a favorite of mine as a child. I loved to do the hand motions as I sang, "Deep and wide/Deep and wide /There's a fountain flowing deep and wide." [7] And then we'd flip the words around and sing, "Wide and deep/Wide and deep/There's a fountain flowing wide and deep."

What is this fountain that we're singing about? **John 7: 37,38** explains: ***"Jesus stood and said in a loud voice, 'Let anyone who is thirsty come to me and drink. Whoever believes in me, as Scripture has said, rivers of living water will flow from within them.'"***

In these two verses, Jesus proclaims Himself to be the place where the living water is found. In other words, He is the fountain. As I researched *fountain* in the Bible, I learned that water (for drinking) is a symbol of the Holy Spirit. It is through the Holy

Spirit that our eyes are opened and we understand our sinfulness. The Holy Spirit reveals to us our need for salvation as He convicts our hearts through His Word. We begin to be so full of Him and His love that His glory overflows from our hearts—like a fountain. He is the *"living water"* that flows deep and wide.

Have you allowed the Fountain to run deep and wide in your life? If not, ask God to give you an unquenchable thirst for Him and to fill you with His Living Water, flavored with love and joy.

Prayer: *You are the Living Water, the Fountain that runs deep and wide in my heart. Keep gushing on me! Soak my heart and my life with Your love. May every area of my life be so saturated with You that I drip, splash, and pour the joy of the Lord into and onto the lives of others.*

Abundant Joy Juice

Have you had your Joy Juice today? I've found that it's a great drink for both children and adults.

As children, many of us learned lots of praise choruses and songs about Jesus. Did you ever sing the song "Jesus Loves the Little Children"? If so, you probably recall the words:

Jesus loves the little children,
All the children of the world.
Black and yellow, red and white,
They're all precious in His sight,
Jesus loves the little children of the world.

As I was looking at the lyrics to this old song, I found that there were verses I'd not learned as a child. These lesser known verses shed a whole new light on the meaning of song. Here are some excerpts from the remaining verses:

Whether you're rich or whether you're poor,
It matters not to Him.

He remembers where you're going,
Not where you've been.

If your heart is troubled,
Don't worry, don't you fret.
He knows that you have heard His call,
And he won't forget.

All around the world tonight,
His children rest assured,
That He will watch and He will keep us,
Safe and secure.[8]

Jesus loves all the children of the world. How true that simple statement is. But do you realize that those "children" are you and me? No matter our age, if we've accepted Him as our Savior and Lord and trusted our Father in Heaven to be in control of our lives, then we are His children. It doesn't matter what color we are, how much money we have, nor what we've done in the past. If we have responded to His call, then regardless of where we are, we can rest in the security of His loving arms. Now that's a joyful place to be!

Prayer: *Father, I am so thankful to be Your child. I can crawl up onto your lap, rest my head upon Your shoulder, tell You my fears, whisper my secrets, and know that You will protect me and lead me down the right path. Thank You for loving me unconditionally.*

Abundant Joy Juice

Have you had your Joy Juice today? It'll make you feel like singing!

One of the favorite songs of my grandbabies is a tune called, "If You're Happy and You Know It." I can remember teaching it to my Kindergarten classes in years past, and it seemed they all loved the song, too. The words remind us that what's in our hearts will show on our faces. Our body language speaks loudly about how we're feeling.

If you're happy and you know it,
Clap your hands.
If you're happy and you know it,
Clap your hands.
If you're happy and you know it,
Then your face will surely show it.
If you're happy and you know it,
Clap your hands. [9]

The song continues with similar verses that tell us stomp our feet and shout, "Hurray!" if we're happy.

Can you imagine a child singing this song without a smile on his face?

What about you? Do you have a song in your heart, or does your body language tell people that you are burdened by problems and concerns? **Proverbs 17:22** says, *"A joyful heart is good medicine, but a crushed spirit dries up the bones."*

None of us can be happy all the time, but remember, happiness is not the same thing as joy. We can still have the joy of the Lord in the midst of trying times. By trusting in Him to take care of us and resting in His protective care, we can experience that indescribable peace and joy. Maybe we should sing, *"If you're JOYful and you know it, clap your hands!"*

Prayer: *Lord Jesus, I know that cannot be happy all the time. You've never promised that every day will be filled with all good things. But You have promised* *to always be with me, and for that, I choose to have a joyful heart. Just knowing that You are there for me in the unhappy times, as well as the good, gives me such peace and joy.*

Chapter Five

✻

Hidden Recipes for Joy Juice

✳

Have you had your Joy Juice today? You need to start each day by faithfully drinking it and serving it—especially in your home.

"Yesterday is history. Tomorrow is a mystery. And today? Today is a gift. That's why we call it the present," said Babtunde Olaunji. [1]

Do you view each new day as a gift from God? We should be seeking guidance in how to live a more godly, productive life every day. Wouldn't it be great if we had an instruction manual to tell us how? Well, good news. We do! It's called the Holy Bible.

Psalm 119: 11 says, *"Thy word have I hid in mine heart, that I might not sin against thee"* **(KJV).** How do we "hide" God's word in our heart? By reading and studying it *often*, by memorizing scripture, and by applying it daily, the Word becomes part of us. When we are so familiar with scriptures that we know them "by heart," we are able to face any situation that may come our way in a godly manner. How? By having the knowledge and truth hidden in the depths of our hearts and minds, our thoughts will default to God's answers and God's perspectives.

As you start the day, realize that this is the day the Lord has made *for you*. It is full of promise. We know that all things won't be perfectly wonderful, but we know the One Who is wonderfully perfect. And He will always be there to guide us. Let's ask the Lord to give us a desire to study His Word. Let's make it our goal to develop a deeper relationship with God through Bible study and prayer. God is always willing to do His part, if we will only do ours.

Joyfully anticipate the opportunities that God will give you today, tomorrow, and in the days to come. When you are sold out to Him and are following His guidelines in the Scripture, you can ***"count it all joy"*** **(James 1:2, KJV).**

Prayer: *Precious Savior, thank you for the gift of today. Indeed, it is a present that's just waiting to be unwrapped. Help me to see the beauty in it, as You have covered it in Your love and tied it with a beautiful bow of joy. Remind me that it's my decision if I simply place it on a shelf and leave it, unopened. Likewise, I can choose to prayerfully pull off the wrapping and enjoy spending time with You as we face the new day together.*

Have you had your Joy Juice today? The great thing about this special drink is that its flavor is new every day.

That reminds me of a scripture in **Lamentations 3:22, 23**: *"Because of the LORD's great love we are not consumed, for his compassions never fail. They are new every morning; great is your faithfulness."*

This is such a comforting, encouraging passage to hide in our hearts, especially when we're trying to put the past behind us. God's love, compassion, and forgiveness can erase our mistakes and give us hope.

Often times, our biggest problem is that we can't forgive ourselves. All of us have made mistakes, bad decisions, and ungodly choices. But nothing is too bad to bring before Him. If we come to Him with a broken heart and we are truly repentant of the sins we've committed, He is willing to give us a new beginning.

Today is the perfect time to get things right with God and ask Him to wipe the slate clean so that you can have a fresh start. Use him as your guide, your compass, your conscience. Let the Holy Spirit prick your heart and give you new goals that will draw you closer to Him and will help you to accomplish His will and purpose for your life.

May I challenge you to memorize **Lamentations 3:22, 23**? Hide these words in your heart, and experience joy in the Lord.

Prayer: *Great is Your faithfulness, Lord. You are the only One in whom I can always trust. Never will You fail me, though many times I have failed You. You continue to love me. Your compassion and Your mercy for me is new every morning. What joy that brings to my heart!*

Have you had your Joy Juice today? When we're drinking our Joy Juice, it increases our appetite for Scripture.

We know that hiding God's Word in our hearts is so important to our spiritual growth and maturity. When we feast on His Word, we become more obedient to His commands and instructions. There are many verses in the Bible that instruct us to obey our Heavenly Father. Let's memorize **Jeremiah 7:23**:

"Obey me, and I will be your God and you will be my people. Walk in obedience to all I command you, that it may go well with you."

God loves us. It's that simple. He wants our life to *"go well"* with us. What is our part in this equation? To *"walk in obedience to all [He] command[s]."* That doesn't mean just going through the motions. It's a matter of the heart. Our love for Him should be so great that we *want* to obey Him. Knowing that He will never ask us to do anything that would harm us should be a motivator to stay steeped in His Word so that we will know His wise commands and instructions. And when we're feeling weak—like we are going to fail—we can call out to Him, and He *will* answer us.

Sometimes we go running to Him like a child jumping into the arms of a loving father. Other times we are so weak that He has to scoop us up off the ground and pull us to his bosom. Either way, we can feel those strong, loving arms around us in every type of situation. Even when the unexpected heartbreak comes, it can ***"go well with [us]"*** because of our relationship with Him. That's what you call a relationship of joy.

Prayer: *Father, it is my desire to walk in Your ways, but I find myself falling very short. May I develop the discipline to study and memorize the Scriptures so that I will have Your Word with me and in me at all times. Then when that challenge comes, I can pull from the well that runs deep within my heart. May I* *fall more and more in love with You every day so that my obedience is an outward display of my love for You and my joy in You.*

Have you had your Joy Juice today? How 'bout a fresh batch today? It's extra tasty when it's freshly squeezed from God's vineyard.

"Oh, taste and see that the LORD is good; Blessed is the man who trusts in him" **(Ps. 34:8, NKJV).** What a verse to hide in our hearts! The Lord has given us five senses, and He tells us in this verse to use two of them to experience His goodness. Both taste and sight are mentioned.

Let's talk about taste first. May I challenge you to an experiment? Try putting anything into your mouth without noticing it. It is just too hard not to notice. When tasting something you enjoy, whether it's a steaming cup of delicious coffee or a ripe, sweet, juicy orange, the sensation of the liquid filling your mouth and passing over those taste buds that God so strategically placed on your tongue is rich indeed. Notice the temperature, the texture, the flavors. Let it linger in your mouth while you enjoy the taste. Thank the Lord for your sense of taste, and thank

Him for His goodness. Ask Him to make you aware of what His goodness tastes like.

Next begin to notice what you *see*. Ask the Lord to show Himself to you through the beauty of His creation: the gorgeous sunrise or sunset, the miracle of a new baby, the burst of color in a bouquet of flowers. Observe your surroundings with a fresh perspective.

Now, thank God for your gifts of taste and sight. Notice how many different ways He communicates His goodness and great joy.

Prayer: *Lord, thank you for my five senses. Make me keenly aware of how You bless me over and over again through these gifts of life that so often I take for granted. May my heart's desire be to taste and see You in everything—from the time I get up until the time I go to bed. And then may I have sweet dreams of joy in You, Lord.*

Have you had your Joy Juice today? Don't hide it from others. Share it!

The past few devotionals have been talking about hiding God's Word in our hearts so that we will be prepared for what each new day will bring. We know that God will always be there for us, but we want to do our part as well. So we're aiming to read, study, and memorize more scripture, right?

We are reminded that God's mercies are new every day; we can depend on His faithfulness. But we must also remember that we are to obey his commands, and we can't obey them if we don't know them. That's why studying and meditating on them is imperative. When we begin to really focus on God, we'll be able to "taste" and "see" that the Lord is *so* good to us. This realization fills our hearts with joy, and we'll want to share it with others.

Mark 16:15 tells us that Jesus said, *"Go into all the world and preach the gospel to all creation."* Who do you think Jesus was talking to? First, he was speaking to his disciples. He was giving instructions for them to tell everyone that He had paid the penalty for their sin and that those who believe in Him will be forgiven and live eternally with God. [2]

But do you realize that the command is for us, too? We, as believers, are disciples of Christ. That means we should be sharing our faith with everyone God brings across our path. Many times we share using words; other times it's our actions and our attitudes that share the Gospel. Showing love, forgiveness, and mercy toward others is a good way to reflect the joy of Jesus.

Prayer: *"Go into all the world!" That's what You've commanded me to do, God. I know that, so why do I often treat this as if it's a suggestion rather than the Great Commission? As I face this day, show me where You would have me serve You. I know that You have divine appointments waiting for me, so please open my eyes and help me to see them. Put Your* *words in my mouth, Your love for others in my heart, and let Your joy radiate from my countenance.*

Abundant Joy Juice

Have you had your Joy Juice today? Be prepared by drinking a healthy portion today, every chance you get.

Don't we wish that solving our problems was as simple as taking a sip, swig, or swallow of a tasty liquid? If only we had a magic potion that would fill our lives with good things and happy times, we'd be content. Right? I'm not so sure.

It seems that we are a selfish breed. No matter what or how much we have, we always want more or something new. I guess that's why the Lord allows challenges to come along. Hard times make our faith grow, and we learn to depend more on Him and less on ourselves.

All of us would probably choose a life overflowing with sweet blessings—good health, happiness, and no major problems—if we had a choice. Let's remove those rose-colored glasses and face reality. There will always be challenges along our path. We may have setbacks—physically, emotionally, financially. We may experience disappointment, hurt, and maybe even devastating heartbreak. But do you understand that even in the midst of reality we can still have joy in the Lord?

I will continue to remind you that joy and happiness are not the same. We're not happy when that painful circumstance comes into our lives, such as the loss of a loved one, the diagnosis of a disease, the end of a relationship, or a financial struggle. Those are not happy times. Nevertheless, a relationship with the Lord produces joy as **Psalm 145:18, 20** reminds us: *"The LORD is near to all who call on him, to all who call on him in truth. The LORD watches over all who love him."*

Hide that truth in your heart. Our Lord is near and loves us. All you have to do is call on Him, and He will joyfully answer.

Prayer: *Father, You have told me in Your Word that You are near to those who call. So I am calling on*

You now. Please watch over me and my family. Draw us closer and closer to You with each passing day. Especially when circumstances seem impossible and I can't see the good, give me a new glimpse of You in that situation. Help me to see through Jesus-colored glasses, a perspective which magnifies Your love and joy.

Have you had your Joy Juice today? Even if you are hurting (especially if you're hurting), you need to drink in the Joy Juice of Jesus.

Many people believe in God only when they are prospering. They think that if God is a loving God then He will not let bad things happen to them. Some feel that suffering is God's judgment for sin, but this is not always true. Suffering *is* sometimes God's way to teach, discipline, and refine, but this is an incomplete explanation. God wants us to realize that we can always trust Him for Who He is.

When you feel that your burdens are heavier than you can possibly bear, please be reminded that you are never alone. Sometimes we get to our breaking point, and we want to yell, "It's not fair!" But what we have to realize is that God is going to do what He knows is best, regardless of what we think is fair. It is far more important to note that God continually demonstrates His love and care. Sometimes we are just so focused on our problems that we miss the many blessings that are ours each day.

Remember Job in the Old Testament? This man knew what suffering meant. He lost *everything*, but the scriptures tell us that he fell to the ground in worship and said, **"Naked I came from my mother's womb, and naked I will depart. The LORD gave and the LORD has taken away; may the name of the LORD be praised"** (**Job 1:21**).

Job obviously drank His Joy Juice consistently. Let's follow his example and do the same.

Prayer: *Father God, I confess that many times I get selfish and want what I want when I want it. Often I see things as unfair, especially when my prayers go seemingly unanswered or something unexpected happens. May Job be my role model as he gave You praise, even when he lost everything. Lord, help me to be satisfied with what You have given me and for Your plans.*

Have you had your Joy Juice today? Drinking it faithfully will help you to grow as a Christian and become what God intended you to be.

There is a legend of a Cherokee Indian youth's rite of passage:

His father takes him into the forest, blindfolds him, and leaves him alone. He is required to sit on a stump the whole night and not remove the blindfold until the rays of the morning sun shine through it. He cannot cry out for help to anyone.

Once he survives the night, he will be a MAN. He cannot tell the other boys of this experience, because each lad must come into manhood on his own.

The boy is naturally terrified. He can hear all kinds of noises. Wild beasts must surely be all around him. The wind blows hard and shakes his stump, but he sits stoically, never removing the blindfold. It's the only way he can become a man!

Finally, after a horrific night the sun appears and he removes his blindfold.

It is then that he discovers his father sitting on the stump next to him.

He has been at watch the entire night, protecting his son from harm. [3]

Examine the similarities between this story and our relationship with God. Though at times we feel very alone, God our Father is watching over us, "sitting on the stump," right beside us. He is near at all times and waits for us to reach out for His protection and mighty strength. Often we need to be reminded that just because we can't see God doesn't mean that He's not there. Hide the words of **2 Corinthians 5:7** in your heart: ***"For we walk by faith, not by sight"*** **(KJV).**

Prayer: *Sometimes, Lord, I feel like the little boy sitting in the dark as I think I'm all alone. But You are always there. Help me never to forget that. Grow me; strengthen my faith and trust in You so that I will be able to weather every storm, be bold with each new challenge, and rest in the safety of Your protective arms.*

Abundant Joy Juice

Have you had your Joy Juice today? It's made with a secret recipe that's hidden from the world's eye. However, when you discover it, you will be overflowing with the joy of the Lord. It's simply delicious, yet indescribable.

We live in an age of instant everything—instant coffee, microwavable dinners, instant payment by scanning debit and credit cards or paying online. It's almost as if we have forgotten how to wait. We even expect to learn patience *instantly*. (Don't miss that contradiction of terms.)

When we experience pain, whether it is physical or emotional, we want relief quickly. We want an instant cure for everything from headaches to heartbreaks. Some pains can be cured, but the fact is that we live in a world where people are going to suffer. And we never know when it's going to be our turn. Sometimes suffering comes from consequences related to our own bad choices and actions. Other times, suffering shapes us for special service to others. Still other times, we are under attack from

Abundant Joy Juice

the enemy. Most often we don't understand why we have to suffer. At those times, are we willing to trust God in spite of unanswered questions?

In order to be able to face each day with joy, regardless of our circumstances, we must come to the understanding that knowing God is better than knowing why. Remember, pain is not always punishment. God might be using that difficult situation to mold you and make you into the kind of person that He created you to be. His desire and plan is that His purpose can be fulfilled in you and through you. Now, that's a joyful thought.

But he said to me, 'My grace is sufficient for you, for my power is made perfect in weakness.' Therefore I will boast all the more gladly about my weaknesses, so that Christ's power may rest on me. That is why, for Christ's sake, I delight in weaknesses, in insults, in hardships, in persecutions, in difficulties. For when I am weak, then I am strong. **(2 Cor. 12:9, 10)**

Prayer: *Father, I've often been told not to pray for patience. So today I pray that You make me content with Your timing. When my prayers go seemingly unanswered, help me to remember that it's just not time yet or You have something else planned that is so much better. Lord, pain is not an enjoyable thing to have to deal with, whether it's emotional or physical, but let me call out to You in the midst of my suffering and have the faith to trust that You are in control.*

Abundant Joy Juice

Have you had your Joy Juice today? Sometimes we have to make ourselves drink it, even if we don't feel like it.

Wouldn't it be great if life brought nothing but good things? But we know that trials and tribulations are going to come our way. **James 1:2-4 says:**

Consider it pure joy, my brothers and sisters, whenever you face trials of many kinds, because you know that the testing of your faith produces perseverance. Let perseverance finish its work so that you may be mature and complete, not lacking anything.

And then in **verse 12,** James reminds us of our reward: *"Blessed is the one who perseveres under trial because, having stood the test, that person will receive the crown of life that the Lord has promised to those who love him."* What a joyful day that will be—when we receive our *"crown of life."*

Becoming a follower of Christ does not make us immune to life's difficulties on earth. But the scripture teaches us clearly that God *can* and *will* work in the midst of those tough times. The hard part is that we often cannot see God working while we are in that tough, hurtful situation. That's when we must patiently trust, even when we don't feel like it. Trusting God is a conscious decision. And the commitment to stand firm in our faith will cause us to be able to ***"consider it pure joy."***

Let's remember to drink our Joy Juice, even when it doesn't taste sweet, because God guarantees that we *will* experience joy again—in His perfect timing.

Prayer: *May my trials be opportunities for me to see Your faithfulness, dear Lord. When I feel stressed and stretched, help me to see that You will not allow anything beyond what I can handle. May I grow and become spiritually mature and complete, just as the* *scripture says. Give me courage and boldness to stand the test and come out on the other side, overflowing with joy from You.*

Chapter Six

❋

Dreaming of Joy Juice

Have you had your Joy Juice today? Maybe you like it so much that you even dream about it.

Are you a dreamer? I'm not talking about dreaming when you are asleep. Do you have something that you've always wanted to accomplish? Maybe it's a goal that you carry in your heart and you find yourself thinking about it often—wishing and hoping that one day you'll be able to fulfill that desire.

I believe that we all have dreams. Some of you know exactly what your dream is; others may not have discovered yours yet. But God has created each of us with certain strengths, likes, desires, and passions that make us unique. Don't you think He intends for us to use these special qualities?

Ask God for wisdom about how to accomplish the dream He has placed in your heart. He wants us to call out to Him for direction and guidance. He may be waiting on you to ask. **Proverbs 3:6** instructs us: *"In all thy ways acknowledge him, and he shall direct thy paths"* (**KJV**).

So the first step to accomplishing your dream is to acknowledge God. Then, step out on faith and live for Him, trusting Him in all that you do. When you determine to walk daily with Him, your dream of serving Him with your talents, abilities, and passions will become a reality. God will do His part, but we must be willing and ready to do ours. When you get to that place where you are living your dream, it will be like snuggling up to a beautiful pillow of joy.

Prayer: *Father, just the thought of snuggling up close to You brings me a comfort and calmness. I do* *have a dream, and I confess that I think about it a lot. But You already know that because You are the One Who implanted that dream in my heart. Please give me wisdom, direction, and guidance to pursue the dream, and may it be used as a ministry to draw others to know You.*

Abundant Joy Juice

Have you had your Joy Juice today? Our Heavenly Father has created a special flavor just for you. He has created each of us in a unique way so that His purpose can be accomplished in us and through us. He has put a dream in our hearts. Have you discovered your dream?

If you've ever found yourself thinking, "I wish I could do more with my life," you're not alone. If you've ever had the idea that there might be something that you're missing, then God might be nudging you toward that dream that He has placed in your heart.

Author Cindy McMenamin writes in her book *When a Woman Discovers Her Dream* that "there are two kinds of people when it comes to discovering one's dreams: those who dare to dream and those who have given up." [1]

Which are you?

Paul teaches us in **Philippians 1** that we need to learn to be content in the midst of our circumstances. But he goes on to tell us that we should

"press on toward the goal to win the prize for which God has called [us] heavenward in Christ Jesus" **(Phil. 3:14).** Doesn't that sound as if we are to keep pressing toward accomplishing the dream God has given us? Only when we begin prayerfully to consider and intentionally to pursue that dream will God begin to show us His plan.

Let's not miss out on the many opportunities of joy He intends for us! Be available, and He will guide you and equip you. Dare to dream, but make sure those dreams are from the joyful Dream-Giver.

Prayer: *Open the eyes of my heart, Lord, that I may see and understand Your purpose for my life. Give me clarity to know which dreams are from You and which are not Your best for my life. Help me to press on in Your strength—not my own—knowing that it is only through Your blessing and guidance that this dream can become a reality.*

Abundant Joy Juice

Have you had your Joy Juice today? It will bring joy to our Heavenly Father if we drink it faithfully.

Do you realize that we bring joy to our Father when we are living out the dream that He placed in our hearts? I agree with author Cindi McMenamin who writes the following:

Fulfilling our dream is not really about making ourselves happy. It's not even about feeling significant or gratified. It's not for the admiration or praises of other people. Those are benefits of the living out our dream, but that's not what's important. Our motivation should be to fulfill the call that God has placed on our lives…for His glory! [2]

In **Matthew 22:37** we are told about our primary calling, and that is to **"*love the Lord your God with all your heart and with all your soul and with all your mind.*"**

McMenamin goes on to explain that *this primary calling will be manifested differently in each individual, based on his/her unique dreams. Our secondary or specific calling is how we carry out our expression of love for God—through our thinking, speaking, living and acting entirely for Him. We can't separate the dream from the One who has whispered that dream into our heart. If there was no Dream Giver, there would be no dream.* [3]

May I challenge you to think back to your childhood? What did you really want to be when you grew up? Is that dream still in your heart today? Then it may be God's plan for you. Let's give our dreams to Him. After all, He is the One who planted it in the garden of our heart. As we pursue a closer walk with Him, He will water that dream seed and help it to grow until it comes to fruition. Oh, what a joyful day that will be!

Prayer: *Oh, precious Dream Giver! Thank you for planting the dream deep within my heart. Now, bring it to the forefront of my mind, make it a burning desire of my heart, and give me the creativity and fortitude to follow it through. Guide me every step of the way. May I not get one step ahead nor lag one step behind, but let me stay right in step with You.*

Have you had your Joy Juice today? Or are you rushed and dreaming of when you can slow down long enough to enjoy it?

Busyness is such a distraction at times, isn't it? We have such good intentions of pursuing our goals and dreams, and then we find ourselves so busy with the urgency of life that we just don't have the time to follow through. Our dream is destroyed—or at least put on hold.

I truly believe that if God gives us a dream, He wants to help us realize the dream. We need to be aware of those stumbling blocks along the way. Author Cindi McMenamin calls them "dream destroyers." Let's talk about a few of these:

- Fears and doubts—otherwise known as "negative self-talk" or discouraging thoughts—come against our dreams. To combat these, we need to do as **Philippians 1:6** tells us and "*[be] confident of this, that he who began a good work* *in you will carry it on to completion until the day of Christ Jesus."*

- Another destroyer is discouragement from others. Many times people downplay our dreams in the name of trying to protect us from disappointment. But we need to surround ourselves with cheerleaders who are strong prayer warriors and want God's best for us.
- And then, of course, the main dream destroyer is old Satan himself. He tries to work through our circumstances to dissuade us from our dream. He wants us to give up! [4]

Be encouraged by the verse in Psalm 37:5 which says, *"Commit your way to the LORD; trust in Him."* The Message translation of this verse reads as follows: *"He'll validate your life in the clear light of day and stamp you with approval at high noon."*

Doesn't that just fill your heart with joyful anticipation? Dream big, and trust God to guard you against these destroyers.

Prayer: *Father, help me to be discerning and aware of the dream destroyers in my life. Remind me continually that You have given me this dream, and together we must strive to bring it to fruition. I cannot do it alone! I need You! Speak to my heart; shine Your light on my path, and show me Your way toward accomplishing this dream—our dream.*

Have you had your Joy Juice today? Dream big, and drink a double portion of God's joy.

When we are in the center of God's will, fulfilling His call on our lives, we do indeed drink in the joy that comes from serving Him. So many of us never attempt anything for God because we don't think we're talented enough or smart enough or gifted enough. God plants a dream in our heart, yet we still think, "Oh, sure, God! That's a great idea, but you need to find someone else better qualified."

Throughout the Bible, we read of many who heard God's call but didn't think they were qualified to fulfill it. Remember Queen Esther who was approached by her cousin Mordecai to plead before the King for the lives of the Jewish people? At first she felt very inadequate and afraid. But then she was reminded by Mordecai: ***"Who knows but that you have come to your royal position for such a time as this?"*** **(Esther 4:14)**

Is God calling you for *"such a time as this"*? What dream has He laid upon your heart? If you're not sure, seek His guidance. If you are sure, then step out in faith. He will guide you every step of the way and even give you the boldness that you may need. When He knows you are serious about fulfilling that dream and are trusting in Him completely, He will open doors and turn other people's hearts to help you with that dream.

When Esther agreed to put herself in the position where God could work through her, she accomplished more than she could have ever imagined, and she went down in history as the Queen who saved her people. What legacy will you leave? Let's pray that it's a godly one—filled with joy.

Prayer: *Lord Jesus, I feel the excitement bubbling up in my heart and soul. You have rekindled the spark that I thought was gone. Thank You for reminding me of the dream, and now, I give it totally to You. I give myself to You as a willing vessel through which that* *dream will come to fruition. Oh, the joy I feel in You today! Yet, I know it is nothing compared to what I will feel when I hear You say,* **"Well done, good and faithful servant!"** **(Matt. 25:21).**

Have you had your Joy Juice today? Is there a right way or a wrong way to drink it?

Throughout the Bible, we are given instruction about which way to go. Much wisdom can be found in the pages of God's Word. In **Isaiah 30:21** we read, ***"Whether you turn to the right or to the left, your ears will hear a voice behind you, saying, 'This is the way; walk in it.' "***

Do you recognize God's voice when He is trying to show you the way? Do you hear his counsel regarding the dream He has placed in your heart or a big decision that you need to soon make? In this passage from Isaiah, the people of Jerusalem had left God's path, and he had to correct them. He will do the same for us today, but we must be willing to listen and follow his voice of correction.

When Judah was prosperous and comfortable, they wouldn't listen to God. So He allowed them to go through times of adversity and affliction. The result: they began to listen to God and be guided by Him again. It's always better to be uncomfortable and in tune with the Lord than to be comfortable and out of step with God.

Many times we are going to experience painful trials. But we must remember that God always acts out of his love for us. Next time you go through a difficult time, try to grow from the experience, learning what God wants to teach you. God may be showing you his love by patiently walking with you through adversity and pointing the way—one step at a time.

Prayer: *Master, I must admit that I do **not** like the tough times. Difficult circumstances stink! But I trust that You are with me in the rough situations as well as the good. I am reminded that nothing comes to me without first passing through You. Help me to understand that You are teaching me, pruning me, and shaping me into the creation You intend for me to become. I am taking Your hand and asking You to walk with me through every circumstance—both good and bad. Help me to face each situation with joy, knowing that You are there with me.*

Abundant Joy Juice

Have you had your Joy Juice today? It's the only way to find genuine joy!

You do want genuine joy, don't you? Sadly, people often try to find joy and happiness in the wrong things, such as material possessions, social status, power, or prestige. They may even pursue a dream that's really not God's best for them. They go forward without His leading. They are simply pursuing happiness.

No amount of worldly success, possessions, or achievement can bring us true joy. There is only One Way. You'll find it by reading **John 14:6.** This verse comes straight from the heart and lips of Jesus: *"I am the way and the truth and the life. No one comes to the Father except through me."*

My Bible footnote elaborates: "As the *way*, Jesus is our path to the Father. As the *truth*, he is the reality of all God's promises. As the *life*, he joins his divine life to ours, both now and eternally!" [5]

If you feel lost and don't know which way to turn, cling to the truth that Jesus will not only lead you and show you the way, but He *is* the way. Of course, we have to accept Him as our leader and let Him have complete control of our life. Our world offers us all kinds of substitutes, and they might make us happy for a short time. Nevertheless, happiness is not the same as joy. Happiness depends on what's happening; joy depends on Jesus. Nothing or nobody can promise to *always* be with us as the Way, the Truth, and the Life. No one, that is, except Jesus.

Prayer: *You are the Way. You are the Truth. You are the Life. You are the Way. You are the Truth. You are the Life. You are the Way. You are the Truth. You are the Life.*

If it takes me a thousand times to repeat this for it to seep deep, deep into my soul, my heart, my consciousness, then so be it. May I face the day with the joy found only in You as I trust you to show me the way, reveal to me the truth, and discover the abundant, joyful life found in only in You.

Abundant Joy Juice

Have you had your Joy Juice today? It's the perfect drink if you want to discover the joyful way of life. Dare to dream because you have God on your side.

I still recall the feeling of desperation and panic that I felt as a little girl when I strayed away from my mother in a large department store one day. As I turned to find my mother, she was not there. Due to the huge crowd and my small size, as hard as I tried, I could not see my mom. I thought I was lost. Tears began to well up in my eyes, and I was just about to scream when my mother placed her loving hand on my shoulder, and I realized that she had never lost sight of me. She was only a few feet away, watching me the whole time. I had no reason to be so frightened and upset.

Do you ever panic because it seems that the Lord has forgotten about you? Are you running around, trying to find him, wondering where He has gone? Take a deep breath and calm down. He hasn't gone anywhere! He's right there with His eyes focused precisely on you. Many times it's *we* who have wandered away from the path, but He always knows where we are and will help us—if we will allow Him. His Word tells us over and over again that we can trust in Him. He is near. He loves us.

In **Psalm 18:30** we receive comfort: *"As for God, his way is perfect: the LORD's word is flawless; he shields all who take refuge in him."*

"His way is perfect"—though we will never be! We can take refuge in our perfect Savior. Doesn't that soothe your fears and wash you with a sweet, joyful peace? Now, dare to dream the seemingly impossible dream because nothing is impossible when you put your faith in God.

Prayer: *Oh, dear Father. I am so flawed, so imperfect. Yet You love me just the way I am. You are my Creator, and You know the dreams of my heart as well as my limitations. In my imperfection, I can draw much strength from the power of Your perfect will. Lead me, guide me, and make clear to me my next step in Your Master plan for my life.*

Have you had your Joy Juice today? It's the best way I know to keep a joyful outlook on life and pursue the dreams God has placed in your heart.

Many times we have major decisions to make, and we just don't have a clue which way to go. Maybe the decision is between two good things. That scenario makes it extra difficult to discern what's best. It could be that no matter what decision we make, someone is going to be hurt or disappointed.

During times of decision making, we get unsolicited advice from well-meaning friends. That input only seems to confuse us more. How do we know to whom to listen? Well, there is One we can always trust to guide us and help us make the best decisions. Listen to the reassuring words of God in **Psalm 32:8:** *"I will instruct you and teach you in the way you should go; I will counsel you with my loving eye on you."*

Our Heavenly Father desires to instruct us and teach us the right way. He has given us the best instruction manual and guidebook ever written: The

Holy Bible. Like a good student who has to discipline himself to study for exams, we should be diligent in studying the Scripture so that we will be able to pass any test of our faith. He promises to counsel us and watch over us, but we must be obedient to His leading and follow His instruction.

Let's determine to study the Bible, our instruction manual, so that when test time comes, we will pass with flying colors. May our Master Teacher be joyfully pleased with our obedience and our faithfulness.

Prayer: *Father, Your Word tells us to* ***"study to shew thyself approved"*** *(****2 Tim. 2:15, KJV****). Give me an insatiable appetite for the Scripture; let me develop an unquenchable thirst for the Joy Juice of Jesus. Fill my heart and my mind with the truths found only in Your Holy Word so that when decision time comes, I can apply Your wisdom to my life.*

Abundant Joy Juice

Have you had your Joy Juice today? Forming a good habit of drinking it daily is a sure way to focus on a life of joy.

Developing good habits is not really that hard to do. Do you agree? It's simply making up one's mind and then sticking with it. The Greek Philosopher, Aristotle, said, "We are what we repeatedly do. Excellence then, is not an act, but a habit." [6]

Think about the habits that you've developed over the years, both good habits like brushing your teeth and bathing every day and bad habits like eating fattening snacks before bedtime. Our days are filled with habitual behaviors—some positive and some *not*. But the fact is that we choose our habits.

Have you ever thought about praying about your habits? Prayer, itself, is a good habit; one of the best I know. We can rely on God to fill us with wisdom and joy—if we will get into the habit of always going to Him first. In **Proverbs 4:11**, God gives us the following promise: *"I instruct you in the way of wisdom and lead you along straight paths."*

That verse makes wisdom seem so simple, doesn't it? But we are in a battle because our enemy is out to destroy our good, godly habits by tempting us in our weak areas. Satan wants to discourage us from following the dream that God has placed in our hearts: *"Your enemy the devil prowls around like a roaring lion looking for someone to devour. Resist him, standing firm in the faith"* (**1 Pet. 5:8, 9**).

Standing firm in our faith is a wonderful habit that is imperative for us to develop if we want to walk in His ways. With God's help, we can practice His wisdom and joy until these attributes become a natural part of our life.

Prayer: *Dear God, I confess to You that I so often move forward without asking for Your guidance. Remind me to always seek your wisdom and direction, no matter how big or how insignificant the decision. Show me which step comes next in pursuing the* *dream, the dream You have placed in my heart. Place a hedge of protection around me so that the enemy cannot destroy, devour, or discourage me. Help me to stand strong!*

Chapter Seven

�֍

Household Uses for Joy Juice

�֎

Have you had your Joy Juice today? It's packaged mighty conveniently. And if you think about it, you'll see that it's so handy to have around the house. There are many uses for it, and it's always available.

We are blessed to have many household conveniences these days. I'm afraid I've become dependant on many of my appliances. We take them for granted when they are working well, but when they begin to sputter or quit, we get agitated and can't wait to get them fixed or get a new one. (Or is that just me?)

Take the washing machine for example. That poor contraption gets a workout in most homes almost every day of the week—especially in large families. When we need clean clothes, we can just throw our

Abundant Joy Juice

laundry in the washing machine and assume that it will fill with water, spin, and rinse—just like it was made to do. It gets little thanks from us when it does its job properly. But, boy howdy, do we ever get bent out of shape when it doesn't!

Let's consider this frustration. Do I see a correlation here between the washing machine and God? I sure don't mean to be irreverent, but how many times do we take the blessings of our Heavenly Father for granted? When He's giving us what we think we need and life is good, we often forget the source of those blessings. Seldom do we thank Him enough for the countless blessings that are ours each day. But when our life is interrupted by some unexpected inconvenience, we automatically want to blame God and get agitated that He's not working right.

The truth is that we never have to call a repairman where God is concerned, for He *is* The Repairman. **1 John 1:9** tells us so: *"If we confess our sins, he is faithful and just and will forgive us our sins and purify us from all unrighteousness."*

Run to your spiritual laundry room right now, and see if your washing machine is filling up with the Joy Juice of Jesus.

Prayer: *I confess, Lord, that I do take Your many blessing for granted. Help me to thank You more and complain less. Show me all I have to be thankful for; let me not focus on the things I don't have. Give me a grateful, joyful heart, and let it radiate to others as I go throughout the day.*

Abundant Joy Juice

Have you had your Joy Juice today? Throw a handful of fruit into the blender for a delicious, fresh serving of juice this morning.

Our lives are much like a kitchen blender—whatever we allow into the pitcher greatly influences the end product. If we want a fresh fruit smoothie, we know to put in delicious strawberries or peaches or bananas—whatever suits our taste buds. If we want a milkshake, we scoop up some ice cream and the flavoring of our choice. But what if we decided to put in used coffee grounds, rotten potatoes, and trash? We'd still get an end product, but it would not be anything we'd want to drink or serve.

Do you realize that's exactly what we do when we go to R-rated movies or watch inappropriate things on television? When we listen to music that has lewd and vulgar language in the lyrics and when we listen to cursing and swearing, we are putting trash into our blender of lives. The reading material we choose can adversely affect our thinking, our actions, and our choices. In other words, what we put into our brains comes out as a part of who we are, blended into the whole.

What are you putting into your life blender today? May I suggest adding the Fruit of the Spirit found in **Galatians 5:22, 23?** Consider these ingredients: ***"But the fruit of the Spirit is love, joy, peace, forbearance, kindness, goodness, faithfulness, gentleness and self-control."***

With fruit as delicious as that, the end product will have to be "scrump-dilly-iciously" joyful!

Prayer: *Father, remind me to allow You to be the Master Chef in my kitchen of life. Help me to clean my blender and get ready to mix up batch after batch of delicious Joy Juice flavored with the sweet Fruit of the Spirit. May I have countless opportunities to share it with others.*

Abundant Joy Juice

Have you had your Joy Juice today? Do you like the microwave recipe or the kind you make in the crock pot?

If we took a survey, I believe that most of us would admit that we don't like to wait. We know what we want, and we want it *right now*. We live in the age of fast food, speedy technology, and the microwave.

Sometimes, however, God puts us in the crock pot. He makes us wait and wait and wait. We pray and ask Him for quick interventions in our problems or desires. We even spell out exactly how He should answer our prayers at times—as if He needs our help. But instead of a quick result, we often find ourselves stewing, steaming, and slowly cooking.

God knows that many times the end product will be so much better with time. It takes certain conditions for us to become tenderized and ready. Lots of times it's the slow, steady heat that "cooks" us into the delightful recipe that He knows we can become— if we'll just stay under His constant supervision. He will season us with the right spices of life and add the proper amount of tears and joy to accomplish His delicious end product.

Though microwaves are extremely convenient and helpful when we're in a rush, the old, trusty crock pot usually cooks up a much tastier meal. So let's be patient when God doesn't instantly give us what we ask. As **Psalm 37:7** tells us: *"Be still before the LORD and wait patiently for him."*

Prayer: Heavenly Father, though I don't like the "slow cooker" style of life, I realize that You do know what's best. In those times when it seems as if You are not answering my prayers, help me to be patient and try to learn the lesson You are trying to teach me. Indeed, I do want the very best recipe. May it include a huge serving of joy!

Abundant Joy Juice

Have you had your Joy Juice today? Open the refrigerator, and see if you've got plenty of cool juice prepared for this busy day.

How many times do we go to our refrigerator to get something for a snack or a meal? It sits there working for us all day and all night, for days, weeks, and years on end. Most refrigerators have a freezer which allows us to save food for months. But as nice as our refrigerators are, there is *no way* we can get them to cook our food. They are not made to do that. Their purpose is to keep things cool.

Many times we find ourselves trying to be like someone else. We compare ourselves to them: their skills, their talents, their abilities. We get discouraged because we just don't measure up to them. We can't do what they can.

Let's go back to the refrigerator again and pull out a nice, cold bottle of Joy Juice. You see, just as the frig is made for a specific purpose, so are we. Our purpose is not like anyone else's. Some of us are gifted in one area, while even our family members and close friends have totally different gifts and talents. **1 Corinthians 12:4-6** says it best:

There are different kinds of gifts, but the same Spirit distributes them. There are different kinds of service, but the same Lord. There are different kinds of working, but in all of them and in everyone it is the same God at work.

When we seek God's purpose for our lives, we will be exercising our gifts with joy. And that's a "cool" place to be.

Prayer: *Father, I know it's human nature to compare ourselves with others and want to be able to do or have what someone else has or is able to do. Help me to be satisfied with how you made me; then inspire me to pursue developing those abilities that You created in me. Show me Your purpose for my life. I know it's to glorify You in everything I do, but show me how by using my own individual "joyful flavor."*

Abundant Joy Juice

Have you had your Joy Juice today? Let's mix up an extra special recipe.

Pull out your mixer and follow the directions. I've found a yummy recipe that I am so excited about sharing with you. It's called "Joy Juice Jubilee" and it's sure to please everybody's taste buds.

First you're going to need to make sure your mixing bowl is clean by using **Psalm 51:10:** *"Create in me a pure heart, O God, and renew a steadfast spirit within me."*

Then turn to **Colossians 3:12-15,** and you'll find the list of ingredients that makes this creation so enjoyable. In your heart-shaped mixing bowl, add generous portions of:

- *Compassion*
- *Kindness*
- *Humility*
- *Gentleness*
- *Patience*
- *Forgiveness*

- *Peace*
- *Thankfulness*

Let's see, there seems to be something missing. Oh, I know! It's the sweetening that gives it that irresistible flavor...and that is a double scoop of *love*. Now, gently mix all the ingredients together and pour into your pure heart that has already been prepared. As the flavors melt and blend together, you'll notice a sweet aroma. This recipe is extra good when you garnish with fruit—the Fruit of the Spirit that is. I'll bet you can guess my favorite: the fruit of **joy.**

Prayer: *May I be a "sweet smelling savour" to You, Lord. (Ephesians 5:2, KJB) As I allow You to clean my heart and pour in all those wonderful attributes listed in Colossians 3:12-15, please stir up a joy beyond measure that will ooze out onto others and fill them with the Joy Juice Jubilee that comes from knowing Jesus.*

Abundant Joy Juice

Have you had your Joy Juice today? It's a handy drink to sip on as you do your laundry and other chores.

All of us have chores, different tasks at different times. But one we all have in common is the task of washing our dirty laundry. Regardless of who ends up with that duty in your house, the fact is, it's not always a fun task.

As I opened the cabinet over my washing machine one morning, I began to look at some of the products I had purchased. The shelf was lined with an assortment of things that promised to help remove the soil from my clothes. As I read the names on the bottles and boxes, I began to smile. It occurred to me that Joy Juice is our product of choice when we have spiritual laundry to do.

As I turned on my washing machine, I pulled my Gain washing detergent from the shelf and added it to the tank. Pretty soon, my clothes came out clean and smelling so much fresher that when they had gone in.

In much the same way, we need to get the dirt and stinky grime out of our lives. We should allow

God to spiritually put us through His cleansing. He uses Gain, too. Just look at what He promises we will "gain" when we give our life to Him:

- We will GAIN His forgiveness for all our sins.
- We will GAIN eternal life.
- We will GAIN an inheritance by becoming His child and heir, for in **James 2:5** we read: *"Has not God chosen those who are poor in the eyes of the world to be rich in faith and to inherit the kingdom he promised those who love Him?"*

Have you done your spiritual laundry? Pull out the Joy Juice of Jesus and let Him begin the cleansing process now.

Prayer: *Father, I give myself to You. Please take me, cleanse me, and show me what all I have gained by allowing You to be the top priority in my life. When I* *soil my life by leaving You out of my decisions (which leads to making poor, often ungodly, choices), show me where I have fallen short and give me the faith to turn it all back over to You.*

Abundant Joy Juice

Have you had your Joy Juice today? When you drink it all up, there's always more where that came from.

The word *all* is used in all kinds of ways. We all probably overuse the word at times. We say things like, "I didn't sleep at all last night." What we really mean is that we didn't sleep well. Most of our children have used the famous line, "All of my friends are going!" This really means that some of their friends will be able to go. We all exaggerate by using that word *all* all the time.

There's even a laundry detergent named All. The words on the label compel you to buy the product. It says, "All—small and mighty—3X concentrated—a pure clean for your clothes and skin." I mean, how could you resist such an effective product? 3X more powerful! You should never have a problem with stains again.

We might exaggerate the word and sometimes overestimate the effectiveness of the product, but when it comes down to spiritual truth, the word *all* takes on a whole different meaning. Jesus promises to forgive us of *all* our sins. That's no exaggeration! **1 John 1:9** says, ***"If we confess our sins, he is faithful and just to forgive us our sins, and to cleanse us from all unrighteousness"*** (**KJV**). He also promises take care of *all* our needs: ***"And my God will meet all your needs according to the riches of his glory in Christ Jesus"*** (**Phil. 4:19**).

Give all of your life to Christ! That's how to find abundant joy in all things.

Prayer: Our prayer today is in the form of a song, "Jesus, You're All I Need:"

Jesus, You're all I need.
You're all I need.
Now I give my life to You alone;
You are all I need.
Jesus, You're all I need.
You're all I need.

*Lord, You gave Yourself
So I could live.
You are all I need.
Oh, you purchased my salvation
And wiped away my tears.
Now I drink Your living water,
And I'll never thirst again.
For You alone are Holy;
I'll worship at Your throne,
And You will reign forever.
Holy is the Lord.* [1]

Have you had your Joy Juice today? If you spill a little on your clothes, don't worry. It doesn't stain!

After church on Sundays, my husband and I often go out to eat with friends. More times than not, one of the men will drop food on his tie which leaves a stain. But one couple has learned to be prepared. They carry their trusty Tide to Go stain stick. It promises to get the stain out.

Why is it that we don't like to have stains on our clothes (on the outside), but we don't give a lot of thought to the stains on the inside? Those stains upon our heart called sin have a much greater impact on our lives than a soiled tie or shirt. Maybe because we can't actually see the sin stain with our eyes, we pretend it's not there.

We may be able to hide our sins from other people, but God knows they are there, and He's the One Who really matters. When it comes to removing the stains from our clothing, we often look for the easiest, quickest way, like Tide to Go. But when it comes to confessing our sins, many people don't realize that we've got something so much better. I like to call it the "God to Go" stain remover. It's made with the concentrated Joy Juice of Jesus.

Isaiah 1:18 tells us about the cleansing power of our God: *"Come now, and let us reason together, saith the LORD: though your sins be as scarlet, they shall be as white as snow; though they be red like crimson, they shall be as wool"* (**KJV**).

Use your "God to Go" stain remover by asking our Father to forgive your sins and wash you clean from the inside out. Then get ready to experience the inexpressible joy that comes from experiencing His total forgiveness.

Prayer: *Oh, loving Father, how awesome you are! My sins are many, but Your love is great. Thank You for being a compassionate God that loves me in spite of the mistakes I make. Help me to draw closer and closer to You with each passing moment, and give* *me discernment and wisdom which will protect me from making the same mistakes repeatedly. You are my role model; though I will never be perfect like You, I can be forgiven. What joy floods my soul!*

Abundant Joy Juice

Have you had your Joy Juice today? It will help to *cheer* you; that's for sure.

There are many laundry detergents on the market these days. I don't know where they all got their names, but as you walk the grocery store aisle, observe some of the labels on the boxes and bottles. You'll soon find, as I did, that many of them can be equated with what happens when we let Jesus do our spiritual laundry.

Of course, you probably have guessed that one of my favorite labels on the detergent aisle is the colorful one that boasts the letters C-H-E-E-R! (The dishwashing liquid Joy is my all-time fav!) When we experience the joy of salvation that we can receive only through Christ, we will certainly have a *cheer*ful spirit!

Proverbs 17:22 says it perfectly: *"A cheerful heart is good medicine, but a crushed spirit dries up the bones."* Wouldn't you much rather have a cheerful heart rather than a broken/crushed spirit? And did you know that you can have a cheerful heart even though it's broken? The difference between a Christian with a broken heart and others who don't know Christ is that the Christian leans on the Lord to carry him through the time of heartache. In other words, ***"The joy of the LORD is your strength"*** **(Neh. 8:10)**. When you allow God to comfort you, carry you, and sustain you, He will give you a generous serving of His love and joy.

So, which laundry detergent are you choosing to clean your heart today? I hope it's the one made with the Joy Juice of Jesus. If so, you'll experience a cheerful heart, regardless of your circumstances.

Prayer: *Dear Lord, as I get ready to do my spiritual laundry today, open my eyes to all the dirt and grime in my life. Show me what needs cleaning so that I can pull it from my laundry basket and give it to You. Please wash me and cleanse my life. Give me a* cheer*ful heart of joy!*

Abundant Joy Juice

Have you had your Joy Juice today? Bounce on over to your Bible if you find yourself running short.

The past several devotionals have referred to doing our spiritual laundry. Though we don't like to wear dirty clothes or have stains on our outerwear, sometimes we forget to check the inside for sin dirt. Just as we have to frequently wash our clothes, we need often to do an inspection of our heart. When the grime of daily living is left unattended, the stains become deeper and darker. But there is a simple remedy. It's called *repentance*!

Each and every one of us is a sinner. That's why Jesus came, lived, and died for us. Nothing that we do could pay our sin debt. But, praise God, Jesus has paid it all! When you ask Him to remove the stain of sin from your life, you will be like a new creation: ***"Therefore, if anyone is in Christ, the new creation has come: The old has gone, the new is here!"*** **(2 Cor. 5:17).** Doesn't that make you want to bounce with joy?

Let's think about our laundry once more. When the dirty clothes go through the soapy wash cycle and are rinsed and spun, then it's time to remove them and put them into the dryer. I use a Bounce fabric softener sheet so that when the drying process is complete, our clothes will be soft and sweet smelling. That's what the joy of Jesus does in our lives. When we've asked Jesus into our hearts and He washes away our sin, we'll find our words and deeds much softer and kinder, possessing a sweet aroma and filled with an indescribable joy.

Accept the cleansing power of Jesus and experience the abundant joy that will bounce into your heart. It's guaranteed to add shine to your life as you radiate the love of Christ.

Prayer: *Holy, wonderful God, how thankful I am that You can and will take my dirty sins and wash them white as snow. Add the "softener" to my heart, and give the fabric of my faith that sweet aroma that comes from loving You totally. As I go about my day today, please make my words soft and kind—and full of joy.*

Chapter Eight

※

Garden-grown Joy Juice

Have you had your Joy Juice today? Step out to your garden and gather a fresh batch of the fruit called joy.

Do you have a garden? If not, let's plant one together. I'd like to suggest a joy garden. In **Genesis 2:8** we read about the very first garden: *"Now the LORD God had planted a garden in the east, in Eden; and there he put the man he had formed."*

Admittedly, I am *not* a gardener. I can't even seem to keep a potted plant alive. But I'm determined to plant a thriving *joy garden* that is filled with beautiful fruit that can be shared with others. The first thing gardening experts tell us to do is to dig up the soil and remove the rocks, weeds, and debris. Then, test the soil, and get it ready for the types of plants that you want to grow in your garden.

Our joy garden is a spiritual garden, but in much the same way as an earthly garden, we need to prepare the soil before we can even begin thinking about planting any seeds. Let's dig around in our hearts and find the trash and weeds, such as anger, bitterness, and resentment that will keep the good stuff from growing. We may be holding on tightly to that big old rock of unforgiveness. Nothing will grow in that spot until we clear it completely.

When the soil of our heart is cleaned up and all the unwanted debris is gone, then it's time to test the soil to see if it's ready for planting. Whew, this gardening can be difficult if we try to do it alone. Let's call the Master Gardener and depend on Him to show us how to have a beautiful, healthy garden of joy.

Prayer: *There is so much I could choose to plant in my life garden. Father, help me to select only Your* *best which will lead to joy. Joy comes from rooting my life in You, by planting seeds that will produce good fruit, and by watering it all with prayer. Bless my joy garden, Lord, by shining Your Sonlight on it daily so that I can grow in You.*

Have you had your Joy Juice today? It's just what you need if you're going to be working in your garden.

We've begun tilling our joy garden. We've prepared the soil by removing all the rocks, weeds, and debris. We want to make sure that our hearts are cleansed of all those obstacles that will hinder the fruit of joy from growing. That means getting rid of anger, bitterness, grudges, and unforgiveness. Only with God's help can we release the memories and hurts from the past. And it's a process, one of continual relinquishment to the Master Gardener.

Now that the soil is prepared, the next step is to plant the seeds. Experts tell us that we should always plant the foundational flowers first. As we plant our spiritual garden, we must start with the foundational principles. I interpret that to mean that we need to first plant the seeds of faith, believing in the truth that the Bible is God's inerrant word: ***"All Scripture is God-breathed and is useful for teaching, rebuking,*** *correcting and training in righteousness"* (**2 Tim. 3:16**).

Another foundational seed is the belief that God, the Father, is perfect in holiness, infinite in wisdom, and measureless in power. God showed His love for all people by sending His Son to die for our sins so that we might have eternal life with God in heaven. It is imperative that we plant this truth deep within our hearts and minds. When we get the foundational things planted in our garden, it's easier to see where the other things need to be planted, like the seeds of kindness, compassion, peace, and (of course) lots and lots of joy.

Congratulations on a job well done! It looks as if our garden is well on the way to producing some delicious Joy Juice.

Prayer: *I look to my Master Gardener to lead me today. As I go about "planting," may I use only those*

Abundant Joy Juice

seeds recommended by You, Lord. When the weeds of doubt, fear, discouragement, and anger begin to sprout up, point them out to me quickly so that You and I can pull them up and discard them. I ask for a double portion of the delicious fruit of joy.

Have you had your Joy Juice today? You're gonna need a healthy serving so that we can work in our garden again today.

Speaking of our garden, we've prepared the soil by removing the rocks, weeds, and debris. In our spiritual garden of joy, that means getting rid of unforgiveness, anger, bitterness, and unclean thoughts. When all that is detrimental is cleared away, the good seeds can be planted—seeds such as *love, joy, peace, forbearance, kindness, goodness, faithfulness, gentleness and self-control"* (**Gal. 5:22, 23**).

Next we need to water the newly planted seeds thoroughly, to settle the soil and remove any air pockets. What happens if they don't get water? They'll get mighty thirsty and soon dry up and die. We must be diligent in tending our garden by filling our watering can daily with fresh truth from God's well.

Do you remember the story of the Samaritan woman at the well (**John 4**)? This poor woman had quite a reputation. She had been married five times and was living in sin with a man who wasn't her husband. Her story shows that a well of grace is ready and available to refresh the soul parched by sin and suffering. The woman at the well had her sins washed away. Only Jesus can offer and deliver that kind of mercy. He is the Living Water, concentrated with grace.

John 7:38 says, *"Whoever believes in me, as Scripture has said, rivers of living water will flow from within them."* Let's use that living water generously in our spiritual gardens and watch the seeds that have been planted grow and develop into beautiful specimens of His love and joy.

Prayer: *Living Water, make me thirsty for You. Remind me of Your faithfulness and grace. Rain on me continually with Your mercy, power, and joy.*

Have you had your Joy Juice today? It's chocked full of nutrients because its ingredients are grown in a totally organic garden.

We've heard a lot about organics in recent years. There are organic sections in our grocery stores for those who are striving to eat healthier. Since we're talking about gardens in this chapter, let's consider what organic gardening is all about. This type of gardening means doing things the natural way. No synthetic products, including pesticides and fertilizers, are used. Ideally, organic gardening replenishes the resources as it makes use of them.

Think about your spiritual garden. We know we must prepare our gardens by clearing away the weeds and trash; then comes the planting and watering of the good seeds. We're working in cooperation with God, the Creator, Who "*In the beginning [God] created the heavens and the earth*" (**Gen. 1:1**). We are not to use any man-made products on our gardens that might interfere with God's best.

Often we take charge and try to fix things when our garden isn't producing like *we* think it should. We try to find ways to make it flourish, but often, we mess up the plan and get in the way of God's best.

God's garden manual gives us tried and true tools which will help the seeds of faith to grow in our hearts. Sometimes the Master Gardener throws compost onto our garden that we don't like. But after a while, we realize that it has helped those seeds to sprout and blossom into creations of beauty—joyful outgrowths of something that, at first, was ugly and unwanted. This process teaches us patience, and we grow in faith in the sovereignty of God. Now, that's what you call cultivating a garden of joy in the Lord.

Prayer: *From the beginning, Your garden was beautiful and perfect, Lord. Then man's sin began to mar it. May You guide my thoughts, my actions, and my words so that I can help to spread the fruit of Your* *joy into the gardens of others along my way today and every day. Use me to plant the right seeds which will lead to beautiful spiritual gardens abounding in Your joy.*

Have you had your Joy Juice today? Harvest some from your own personal joy garden. It tastes extra sweet when you've watched it develop before your very eyes.

Thank you for joining me as we co-labor together in our joy gardens. By allowing the Master Gardener to show us what to do, we are assured that the right kinds of things will begin to blossom and grow. If your garden is flourishing, then you've successfully followed His instructions. Here is a recap of joy gardening:

- You've cleaned the garden plot by accepting Him as your personal Savior, allowing him to remove the trash of unforgiveness from your heart. When you realize that God has forgiven all your sins, it will give you a tenderness and new perspective toward those who need forgiveness. Be reminded by **Ephesians 4:32** to *"Be kind and compassionate to one another,* *forgiving each other, just as in Christ God forgave you."*

- Hopefully, you're planting the right seeds by reading the Bible and listening to good Bible teaching (by attending church and studying on your own) and by surrounding yourself with good, godly examples.
- Once those seeds are planted, they need a constant watering. You can't ignore them, or they will wither and die. Be faithful in applying the Living Water to each area of your garden.
- Soon harvest time will come, and you'll be delighted to see how much joy you'll have in your heart when you share with others the fruit of your personal garden. They'll begin to ask how they can have a spiritual garden like yours, and you will be able to boldly share the Joy Juice of Jesus with them.

Diligently and faithfully open the garden of your heart to God. He will joyfully tend it and teach you how to share His joy with others.

Prayer: *Dear God, I know that before you will tend my personal garden, I must invite You in. Though You are powerful and more than able, You wait for the invitation. Please come into my heart and continually remind me of all Your truths that lead to a productive, joyful garden of life.*

Abundant Joy Juice

Have you had your Joy Juice today? Let's lift our Joy Juice glass and toast the joyful, godly dads.

We've been discussing "spiritual gardens." When I think of gardening, my thoughts automatically go to my sweet daddy. Bless his joyful little heart, he loved to garden. But as a child, I despised it. Daddy would plant a summer garden with peas, butterbeans, corn, squash—you name it. And then, he'd turn around and many times, plant a fall garden to boot. He'd expect his children to be just as excited as he was when all the plants began to bud and bloom. Harvest time was great—*if* you liked to pick and shell and gather and can and freeze. (We kids decided that was only fun for adults.)

My father has been deceased for several years now, but the memories he "planted" in my garden will be there till the day I join him and Jesus for eternity. And for that I am so thankful.

In the next few devotionals, I'd like to share some of the truths my dad taught me about having joy in the Lord. He lived up to his name: *Pleasant*.

Yes, that was his first name. It was also my grandfather's name; and my brother is the third. Our daddy most often had a smile on his face because Jesus was in His heart. He truly was a *pleasant* fellow!

The most important lesson my siblings and I learned from his example is that Christians should have the joy of the Lord in their hearts at *all* times. The way to do that is to accept Him as your personal Savior and constant companion. Daddy modeled a sincere, genuine faith.

To summarize today's message in one word, I'd have to choose the word *authenticity*. To be an authentic Christian, one is to live every day as a genuine believer—regardless of circumstances. That means being completely sold out to Christ.

Remember the parable Jesus taught in **Matthew 13:24-30**? It's the one about the wheat and the tares. Consider this explanation of that parable:

Young tares (weeds) and young blades of wheat look the same and can't be distin-

guished until they are grown and ready for harvest. Tares which are symbolic of unbelievers and wheat (authentic Christians) must live side by side in this world. But at harvest time, the tares will be uprooted and thrown away. [1]

We must get ready for the harvest by making sure our faith is genuine and joyful.

Prayer: *Father, thank You for godly earthly dads and the seeds of truth they plant in us. I thank You for being a Father to all of us, ready and willing to guide us. You shine a light on our path in times of darkness and are always there with Your genuine love. May we model ourselves after You.*

Abundant Joy Juice

Have you had your Joy Juice today? Godly fathers have a way of planting delicious seeds of truth into our lives. One way they do this is by the words they speak (or write).

It seems that the art of letter writing is becoming a thing of the past. May I urge you not to neglect this privilege? Not only does a letter bring joy to the person as he/she reads it *now*, but in years to come, it may be a priceless treasure.

That's what recently happened to me. My mother and I were going through some of my dad's keepsakes, and we discovered priceless gems in the form of my daddy's handwriting: notes of things he deemed important, quotes that he'd found along life's path, and personal letters. One such letter he had written especially for his children years earlier (July 30, 1991).

On the pages of that letter were his thoughts, penned from a heart of love, reemphasizing lessons he had taught us by his example. One of the lessons he so beautifully reminded us of was the gift of gratitude. Here is an excerpt from his special letter:

I am so grateful for the many things God has blessed me with, much that I have not earned or deserved. I am grateful for a loving wife and children. You have brought me so much pride and joy. And those grandchildren have given me a new zest for living! I am grateful for good health, good friends, and freedom.

This brief portion of his letter demonstrates that gratitude was a big part of his heart. **Psalm 136:1** could have been his life verse: ***"Give thanks to the LORD, for he is good, for his steadfast love endures forever."***

If you still have your dad, listen to his words of wisdom. If not, recall with gratitude some of the lessons he taught you. You may feel that you've been cheated because your dad was not/is not a godly father. Ask the Lord to heal the hurts in your heart and help you recall some good things that you learned, in spite of the disappointments. Then pass the good along to your children, grandchildren, or young ones in the family. How about putting your uplifting thoughts in writing—in the form of a personal letter? Now, that's a joyful idea!

Prayer: *Thank You, thank You, Father, for the godly role models You have placed along life's path. Thank You for bold men who are not afraid to stand up for Christ and who pass their wisdom and experience along to the young ones under their influence. May I always have a heart of gratitude for the godly examples You have placed in my life. Please use me as an instrument of joy in others' lives, too.*

Abundant Joy Juice

Have you had your Joy Juice today? Honor the godly men in your life by giving them a great big serving of joy!

Once a year on a designated Sunday in June, we celebrate Father's Day. Many of us give gifts and cards to express our love and appreciation. But don't you think that we often take for granted many of the "treasures" good fathers give their families? They work hard, provide for our needs, protect us, and teach us many valuable lessons along the way. In other words, they are planting "seeds" in our "garden of life."

One of the seeds that my own daddy planted in my personal garden was the importance of always finishing what you start. Persevere, even when the going gets touch and you don't *feel* like it. Let me give you an example:

Several years ago, my parents' church was celebrating Homecoming. Since Daddy was one of the oldest living members, the planning committee had asked him to give a little history as part of the program that Sunday morning. Though his health was failing, he appeared to be fine when he first stood to approach the podium. However, after a few minutes into his talk he began to grow weak, his voice faded, and in slow motion his knees buckled and he crumpled to the floor. I can remember the panic I felt! My heart was pounding almost out of my chest as I saw him lying lifeless in front of us.

Thankfully, God was not finished with him yet! A doctor in the congregation rushed to his aid and after a few minutes…with everyone in the church praying…we heard my father's distinctive, yet weak, voice. "Help me up." He gave orders to be seated in a chair on the platform, and then he proceeded to *finish his talk!* He modeled before us **Philippians 4:14: *"I press on toward the goal to win the prize for which God has called me heavenward in Christ Jesus."***

Not only did my sweet, determined daddy plant seeds of perseverance in my garden, but he tended his own seeds so well that they kept producing until the day he died. I'll just bet that he's busy planting all kinds of seeds in heaven's garden today.

Prayer: *Thank You, God, for wonderful, godly earthy fathers. For those who so unselfishly and continually plant healthy seeds into the fruit gardens of their children's lives, I am extremely grateful. Bring to my remembrance many of the things that my own father did for me and how he invested in planting the right kinds of fruit. Show me how to produce those crops in my own life as I share Your joy with others.*

(If you did not have a good Christian father, use this time of prayer to ask God to help you forgive and move forward…maybe even learning from your father's mistakes so that you can make a difference in other's lives.)

Abundant Joy Juice

Have you had your Joy Juice today? When it's produced in our Father's garden, it's extra delicious.

Thank you for allowing me to reminisce about my precious daddy on these past few pages. It has warmed my heart to think of some of things he taught me and my siblings through the years. I've shared with you that he modeled the importance of authenticity, gratitude, and perseverance. Another characteristic that easily comes to mind when I think of godly fathers—including my dad—is the word integrity.

According to Wikipedia, *integrity* is consistency of actions, values, methods, measures, principles, expectations and outcomes. In Christian ethics, integrity is regarded as the quality of having an intuitive sense of honesty and truthfulness. Integrity can be regarded as the opposite of hypocrisy. Simply put, my daddy would say, "Be as good as your word."

As a young gal, I can remember my dad making business deals on his word and a handshake. That was as good as a contract. Isn't it sad that things have changed so much? Why can't we still do business this way? It is because of the lack of integrity we find rampant in our society today.

Proverbs 11:3 wisely warns us: *"The integrity of the upright guides them, but the unfaithful are destroyed by their duplicity."* Don't know about you, but I'm going to be planting seeds of integrity in my joy garden—just as my daddy taught me.

Prayer: *You are a God of integrity! Help me to be more like You every day. Thank You for the seeds that godly models have planted in my life garden. Help me to remember to water those seeds with consistent Bible study, prayer, and worship. As the seeds come to fruition, show me how to make lots of Joy Juice to share with others along the way.*

Have you had your Joy Juice today? Enjoy some as you recall special memories of your childhood.

My childhood memories are filled with lots of laughter and joy. I've already shared with you lessons modeled by my dad, seeds that he planted in my life garden. He taught me how important it is to have an authentic relationship with the Lord, a heart of gratitude, and to persevere even when the going is tough. He showed me how to live a life of integrity. Now, tie all those lessons up with a joyful bow, and you'll discover a valuable gift. It's a treasure, and I sure hope you've discovered it.

My daddy modeled this gift constantly. It's the understanding that we should *enjoy* the journey God has set before us. Enjoyment does not come from the stuff that we accumulate over our life span. Rather, the relationships we invest in make us truly wealthy. And of course, the relationship that should be our top priority is our relationship with God. I quote from a letter my dad wrote almost twenty years ago:

If you notice, most people who seemingly "have it made" are spectators, not participants in life. They look back and yearn for the days when life held greater meaning. It's the journey of life that counts, not the arrival at an (earthly) destination.

If my dad were here today, I think he might add this thought: so, enjoy the journey by spreading the joy of the Lord into each person's garden of life. Time on earth is short, and we must take advantage of every opportunity to tell others about the love and joy of Christ.

Prayer: *Instead of dreading the day before me, give me a new zest and joy for life, Father. Help me to realize that my worth is not about the pursuit of things or how successful I can be by the world's standards. My measuring stick should be how much joy is in my Joy Juice jug...fresh juice squeezed from the Fruit of Your Spirit. Thank You for sharing so generously with me.*

Chapter Nine

✳

Joy Juice:
It's Strangely Divine

Have you had your Joy Juice today? Have you tried offering some to a stranger?

In today's world, we've attached a negative connotation to the word *stranger*. We teach our children not to talk to strangers and certainly never to go anywhere with a stranger. And we do have to be so careful to teach them to beware of those who might not have good intentions. But there are many, many good people in our world that are strangers only because we've never met them.

Recently, I took a trip out of state to attend a ladies' conference. At the beginning of the conference, I knew no one. They were all strangers to me. As the weekend progressed, however, I met many ladies from all over the country who expressed similar interests and a heart for the Lord. Because of our common love for God, we immediately made a connection.

Isn't it wonderful how God can spark friendship? He can take perfect strangers and bring them together in such a way that they feel as if they've known each other for a long time. It's all because of His Love: ***"We love because he first loved us"*** **(1John 4:19).**

Today, I want to challenge you to look for the strangers God puts into your life. It may be that person in the checkout lane at the grocery store, someone you meet at the post office, or a parent of one of your children's friends. Whoever it is, it may be that God has set up a divine appointment. Share His love with that person. Bring joy to them in some small way, and I can guarantee it will come back to you multiplied.

Prayer: *Father, I am so thankful that You are never a stranger. You are as close as a prayer. You watch my every move and know my every need. Thank You for loving me* first. *Oh, how I love You!*

Have you had your Joy Juice today? Keep an extra serving on hand just in case you need it for one of God's divine appointments.

If we are serious about making a difference in our world, about sharing the love and joy of the Lord, then God is going to set up some meetings (otherwise known as "divine appointments"). A divine appointment is exactly what it indicates: an appointment designed by the divine Creator. God is sovereign, all-knowing, all-powerful. He schedules these appointments. Sometimes he wants to bless us; other times, he wants to bless others through us. How many times do we miss our appointments and blessings simply because we're on our own schedule and don't stop to consult The Divine Appointment Maker?

Throughout the Bible, there are many examples of divine appointments. Time after time, God leads the faithful to cross another person's path, and great things happen.

In the book of Esther, we see that she was in the right place at the right time. The scripture says she

"[came] to [her] royal position for such a time as this" **(Esther 4:14).** God used Esther to save the Jewish people, and His covenant with Abraham was upheld. Because of Esther's realization that hers was a divine appointment and because she was willing to be in the center of God's plan, she was blessed with the boldness to stand firm and be used of God in a mighty way that changed history.

Are you willing to be used by God? Ask Him to make you aware of the next divine appointment that he has scheduled for you. An opportunity of joy is waiting for you right around the corner. Don't be late!

Prayer: *Oh, Father. Help me never to be late for the appointments that You have scheduled for me. Give me discernment and wisdom to recognize these meetings as opportunities to share Your love and joy. Bless me with boldness so that You can truly use me* ***"for such a time as this."***

Have you had your Joy Juice today? Be extra sensitive to those who may need some of your Joy Juice. It could even be a stranger who needs a sip or a large serving.

We've discussed on the previous pages about being aware of the divine appointments that God has set up for us. We find many examples of these kinds of meetings in the Bible, one of which we find in **Acts 8**. Philip was in a place where things were popping and hopping. There was a definite moving of the Holy Spirit, yet God called him to leave there and go to the desert. (This is one of those times in which it appeared that God was not making sense.)

Strange as it may seem, God knew what He was doing. Imagine that! And thankfully, Philip trusted Him enough to go as commanded. There in the desert, he would encounter his divine appointment with an important Ethiopian man. God was already preparing the man's heart for this appointment as well. He was sitting in his chariot, reading **Isaiah 53**, which is the prophecy about the sufferings of the Messiah.

God guided Philip to approach the chariot, and he began a conversation with this man. He asked, "Do you understand what you are reading?" That simple question opened the door for Philip to be invited into the chariot and share the Good News. The Ethiopian believed and was baptized. Talk about a successful appointment!

Just as God used Philip, He can use you and me—if we are willing. That stranger that just happens to come into your life today may be your divine appointment. Be sensitive to His leading and share the joy of the Lord with friends and strangers alike.

Prayer: *Father, help me to trust You and follow Your leadership—even when it seems things don't make sense. Show me those You are bringing into my life who need to know about Your saving love today. As I open my mouth to speak, fill it with Your words and then bless those words as they fall upon the ears of each divine appointment. I look forward to being about Your business today.*

Abundant Joy Juice

Have you had your Joy Juice today? Make sure that you have plenty on hand when you entertain strangers.

Entertain strangers? Show hospitality to those you only just met? That sounds strange, doesn't it? But **Hebrews 13:2** says, *"Do not forget to show hospitality to strangers, for by so doing some people have entertained angels without knowing it."*

When we speak of entertaining, we usually think of opening our homes to friends and family for food, fun, and fellowship. But how often have we turned away the opportunity to have someone in our home because we thought it wasn't clean enough or nice enough or because we didn't have time to fix a fancy meal? The truth is that most people don't care how big or beautiful your home is or even what you serve them to eat. They simply enjoy being in a loving and caring atmosphere in which they feel free to be themselves. Very few even notice the dust and spider webs.

We should realize that people are sent into our lives for a reason. They may not always be what they appear to be. Some may be God's special messengers to bless you in a glorious way. Others He may bring to you because He wants to bless them through you.

Will you allow the joy of the Lord to shine through you, even to the strangers of this world? Remember, you are a stranger to some folks, too. But we can all be instruments of His love and joy.

Prayer: *Shine through me, dear Lord. Radiate Your love, joy, peace, and hope as I meet each divine appointment You bring my way. May I be Your ambassador as I meet strangers and love them the way You have modeled.*

Abundant Joy Juice

Have you had your Joy Juice today? May I suggest that you go out of your way today to share some with a stranger?

Strangers come into our lives on a daily basis. When we go to the store, many of the fellow shoppers, clerks, and managers are strangers to us. We sit in church some Sundays with people we don't know on a personal level. As we rush about our busy days, we encounter countless strangers in need of a smile and an encouraging word. Do we go out of our way to share the joy of the Lord with them? Or, do we simply look straight ahead with our own agenda in mind? Many times we don't know what to say, so we say nothing at all.

Consider how many times we have disappointed our Lord by not taking advantage of the divine appointments He has orchestrated for us. Remember that young mother in the check-out lane at the grocery store, the one with tired, fussy little ones? She may simply have needed someone to reach out and help her while she paid for her groceries. We could have demonstrated the compassion of Jesus, but we chose to stay silent.

What about the older gentleman who was having trouble walking from his car into the doctor's office? Should we have offered an extra hand to help him feel steady on his feet and maybe opened that heavy door for him as he entered? We never know when a small act of kindness might be the healing touch that stranger needs to make it through the day.

Ephesians 4:32 was one of the Bible verses many of us learned as children: ***"Be ye kind one to another"* (KJV).** That verse applies to strangers, too, you know. So go out of your way to share God's kindness every day. Have the gift of joy ready for all the divine appointments God has lined up for you specifically.

Prayer: *Help me not to miss my appointments today, Lord. Those divine appointments (that you planned before the beginning of time) should be my priority.*

Abundant Joy Juice

Show me what, where, when, who, and how. Help me to have the servant's heart, ready to obey and serve up some delicious Joy Juice.

Abundant Joy Juice

Have you had your Joy Juice today? Notice the divine fragrance. Why, it smells like fresh flowers on a beautiful spring morning.

We're all familiar with the saying, "April showers bring May flowers." But did you know that this proverb can been traced all the way back to about 1557? Though I've always related it to the literal springtime rains of April, which bring the beautiful flowers of May, one interpretation of the proverb expresses another meaning: "Good things come tomorrow from unpleasant circumstances today." [1]

Immediately when I read this interpretation, my thoughts went to the passage in **James** that comments of suffering:

Consider it pure joy, my brothers and sisters, whenever you face trials of many kinds, because you know that the testing of your faith produces perseverance. Let perseverance finish its work so that you may be

mature and complete, not lacking anything.
(James 1: 2-4)

You may feel as if life has showered you with more than your share of trials. Discouragement and even depression may be sitting heavy upon your chest right now, siphoning all the joy right out of your heart. You might find yourself wanting to yell, "I can't take it anymore!" You need a divine appointment for sure.

By trusting in Him each step of our lives—through the good times and through the trials—godly character will be developed in us. Traits such as perseverance, spiritual maturity, wisdom, and joy will become a part of our character.

So instead of complaining and crying, "Why me?", let's see our struggles as the showers that will bring the flowers of joy into our lives. It might just be that the trial is simply a divine shower which God is using to beautify your flower garden of life and produce some extremely gorgeous bouquets. *"Consider it pure joy"* as you remind others to drink the Joy Juice of Jesus.

Prayer: *Father, I don't always like it when it rains on my parade. However, I do trust You enough to know that You are in control and that You have a plan. Show me that when I am depleting my garden by not growing spiritually (not doing the things I should to continue the growth process), You have to intervene to teach me and develop me. Make my garden grow by allowing the showers along with the flowers, and may I be joyfully accepting of both.*

Abundant Joy Juice

Have you had your Joy Juice today? The natural beauty of wildflowers brings simple joy to so many.

Just the mention of wildflowers turns on the faucet of memories that floods my heart with joyful visions of my precious grandmother. She was so aware of God's intricate detail in all of his Creation. I learned much from her about God's love and how He gives us countless, simple, good things to enjoy. Grandma wasn't rich in material wealth, but she was one of the richest people I've ever known in the joy of the Lord. She would take me on nature walks, and by the time we got home, we'd have our hands full of wildflowers. And of course, we'd be wearing some in our hair. She taught me to find pleasure in God's creation.

Like the wildflowers, God plants unexpected bits of joy into each of our lives, but we have to be watching for them along our walk of life. If our eyes aren't open wide, most often we'll miss them. These blossoms of joy can be found in the strangest places: in a hospital room, at a graveside, in the quiet early morning hours. We might even find these colorful bursts of joy scattered throughout a busy day on the job or driving along with our car full of boisterous youngsters. The key to finding these wildflowers of joy is that our hearts must be prepared to see them. **James 1:12** gives us hope:

Blessed is the one who perseveres under trial because, having stood the test, that person will receive the crown of life that the Lord has promised to those who love him.

Who knows? Our crown might even be decorated with wildflowers as divine symbols of the joy of the Lord.

Let's sip our Joy Juice as we look for beautiful wildflowers along our path today. Pick them joyfully along your way, and share them with others.

Prayer: *Father, I do love You, and I so desire to one day wear the **"crown of life"** that is spoken of in this* *scripture. Though eternity is what is truly important, help me not to be so fixed on what is to come that I miss what is* now. *Show me the natural, beautiful wildflowers of joy on earth that You have planted just for me. Thank You for the gift of my salvation so that I can forever pick the flowers along Heaven's streets of gold when my time on earth is done.*

Abundant Joy Juice

Have you had your Joy Juice today? It's divinely the real stuff—not an artificial substitute.

I attended a wedding not long ago and was impressed by the beautiful flowers. It was not until I got close enough to touch them that I realized that they were not real; they were silk imposters. From a distance, I couldn't tell the difference because they looked authentic. Only close inspection exposed them for what they really were.

I began to ponder how that's true of many so-called Christians. From a distance, they look genuine. But if we get close enough for our lives to touch theirs through everyday activities, we realize that their faith is just a show. It's artificial. They're not at all what they appear to be from a distance.

It's easy to tell "plastic or paper" Christians from the real deal. They may say they love Jesus, but their language, actions, and everyday lifestyle speaks loudly and tattletales on them. The "silk flower" Christians are more difficult to discern. They look really good on the outside. They attend church regularly and may even help with some of the church activities. But if you observe them during the week, you soon see that they don't live any differently from non-believers.

When people look at you, do they see the real thing? Do they see an authentic Christian who loves God with *"all your heart and with all your soul and with all your strength and with all your mind?"* And would your friends, family, and co-workers say that you *"love your neighbor as yourself "* (**Luke 10:27**)? If so, then you are the real thing.

We should all strive to be authentic—divinely filled with joy that blossoms and blooms in others' lives, as well as your own.

Prayer: *I don't want to be paper or plastic, Lord. I want to be real. But many days I fail to be authentic. I let the busyness of my day or my timidity interfere with my actions and words. Fill me with Your bold-*

ness and strength to move past the artificial ways, and help me to surrender completely, 100 percent to You. May I reflect Your love, Your strength, Your compassion, and Your joy.

Abundant Joy Juice

Have you had your Joy Juice today? If you desire to have a strong faith with deep roots, be determined to drink in the joy of Jesus faithfully. Just remind yourself that you have a divine appointment *daily* with your Master.

All of us can probably picture a big, old oak tree standing regal and proud, waving its limbs in the cool breeze as if to say, "Look at me! I'm standing strong after all these years." Oak trees can rise more than 100 feet above the ground and have trunks six to seven feet in diameter. I read about one valley oak in Gridley, California, that had a trunk nine feet in diameter and was more than 600 years old. Wow! That's hard to fathom.

The reason for the strength and longevity of the mighty oak is its root system. Even a young tree has a tap root which can reach 60 feet deep to search for groundwater. As the tree matures, it develops a tiered root system with feeders that permeate different layers in the soil. This system makes it easy to find the water needed for growth; these roots also embed the tree securely in the dirt. Mature valley oaks can produce up to a ton of acorns in a good year.

I don't know about you, but I want to be a mature valley oak tree—spiritually speaking. I want my roots (and I'm not talking about my Lady Clairol roots) to reach so deep that I can always find the Living Water for my thirsty soul. I desire to grow deeper and stronger with age so that I can withstand the storms that inevitably are going to come my way. And I certainly want to be productive and grow much fruit of the Spirit, especially the fruit of joy.

Prayer: *Father, I am planting myself like a mighty oak before You today. Make my roots go deep as I study Your word and apply it to my life. Please water me generously with Your Joy Juice that comes by squeezing truth from the Fruit of the Spirit. May I grow spiritually to the point of being compared to the mature valley oak trees that stand so staunchly. I desire to stand boldly and strongly for You.*

Abundant Joy Juice

Have you had your Joy Juice today? You don't have to wait until a special occasion to drink it or serve it, you know. You can find divine appointments in the midst of routine days if you are sincerely looking for them.

My mother taught me that when I wanted something, I'd have a much better chance of getting it if I asked nicely. So, here goes: would you *please, please, please*—with a cherry on top—strive toward being a consistently joyful Christian? Why? If we would all allow God to guard our lips, guide our steps, and give His joy through us, then this world would be a much better place.

There are many people who pin on their "I'm a Christian" corsage or carry a beautiful bouquet of spiritual clichés to use when the time is right. But when that time of temptation or testing comes, they don't have the genuine faith to make godly choices. They fall right into the trap that Satan has set for them. They give in to peer pressure; they let pride rule their decisions; they get caught up in wanting more, more, more material possessions.

The past several devotionals have been a challenge for each of us to grow into a thriving, joyful Christian who blooms where he is planted. May we become specimens of His love that will attract others to our Creator. Let's live expectantly, looking for the many wildflowers of joy that God has planted along our path. May each of us strive to live an authentic, genuine Christian walk that always matches the talk that comes from a joyful mouth and heart.

But thanks be to God, who always leads us as captives in Christ's triumphal procession and uses us to spread the aroma of the knowledge of him everywhere. **(2 Cor. 2:14)**

Prayer: *As the scripture says, thanks be to God! Thank you, God, my Creator, for the countless dem-*

onstrations of Your love that are before me each day. Help me to fall so deeply in love with You and Your Word that I only want more of You. Material possessions are only temporary. You are everlasting. I want to walk in Your footsteps and be a genuine expression and refection of my Savior, Jesus Christ. Use me as your mouthpiece when and where You so choose. As I go throughout this day, Father, may I remember to sing of Your joy, no matter what comes my way. We can handle it together.

Chapter Ten

✳

Pride and Jealousy: NOT a Recipe for Joy Juice

�֍

Have you had your Joy Juice today? I'm so proud of you if you have!

It's a given that we all like to hear the words, "I'm proud of you!" This is especially true when they come from someone we love and admire. Children in particular need to hear encouraging words. They like to make their parents and teachers proud. In this sense of the word, pride is good.

But often we get snared in the trap of sinful pride. Look closely at the word *pride*. In the very center is the letter *I*. How appropriate! You see, the meaning of sinful pride is preoccupation with self: me, myself, and I.

In **Proverbs 6:16-19** we read the following:

These are six things the LORD hates, seven that are detestable to him:
haughty eyes, a lying tongue, hands that shed innocent blood,
a heart that devises wicked schemes, feet that are quick to rush into evil,
a false witness who pours out lies and one who stirs up conflict in the community.

The number one thing on this list is the sin of pride, described here as *"haughty eyes."* Let's remember that pride is the sin that led Israel to reject all the prophets that God sent to warn them of their evil ways. Pride is the sin that caused the Pharisees to reject Jesus. Pride made the Laodiceans lukewarm and blind to their sin.

Are we so different from those prideful people we read about in the Bible? What's the antidote for this sin sickness? J-E-S-U-S! Let's keep the Joy Juice of Jesus within arms' reach. We never know when we might need to wash down a prideful thought or word and replace it with the fruit of joy.

Prayer: *The verse for today, Lord, reminds me that there are things You hate. Pride is at the top of the list. As I begin each new day, guard my thoughts, my expressions, my words. Separate me from the sin of pride and evil influences. Remind me that I am nothing without You, and I am no better than anyone else. Instead of being the* I *in the word* pride, *help me to always stay focused on the "I" in the word* King. *You are the King of Kings and the Lord of Lords, and that thought should keep me joyfully humble.*

Have you had your Joy Juice today? Let's not get prideful as we drink it.

Though we want to do everything as unto the Lord (**Colossians 3:23**) and strive to do the best we can in every area of our lives, we don't want to become prideful.

Consider what it means to honor God in respect to pride and humility.

*There is a difference between the kind of pride that God hates (**Prov. 8:13**) and the kind of pride we feel about a job well done. The kind of pride that stems from self-righteousness is sin, and God hates it because it is a hindrance to seeking Him.* **Psalm 10:4** *explains that the proud are so consumed with themselves that their thoughts are far from God:* **"In his pride the wicked does not seek him; in all his thoughts there is no room for God."** *This kind of haughty pride is the opposite of the spirit of humility that God seeks.*

*We should strive to be **"poor in spirit" (Matt. 5:3).** That means to recognize our spiritual bankruptcy and our inability to come to God aside from His divine grace.* [1]

So often we stumble because of prideful thoughts. If we do not identify pride as a stumbling block to our spiritual growth, we will fall face first into destruction. Pride is something that each and every one of us has to deal with, no matter how young or old, rich or poor. It does not matter which church or if we attend. **Proverbs** tells us that pride breeds quarrels **(13:10)**; it leads to disgrace **(11:2)**, punishment **(16:5),** and destruction **(16:18)**. It inevitably ends in downfall **(18:12)**.

May each of us be ***"poor in spirit"*** so that we will inherit the kingdom of God. What a joyful day that will be!

Prayer: *Father, I know in my head that I should not be prideful, but in my heart, I realize that many times* *my actions reflect a prideful spirit. Show me how to be humble and **"poor in spirit."** My desire is to live a joyful life for You and in You—on earth and for eternity. And I know that requires putting aside my pride and selfish desires. I trust You to walk with me every step of the way.*

Have you had your Joy Juice today? Yes? Well, I'm glad, but let's not be prideful about it.

There are many references to pride throughout Scripture. Often we are warned about the consequences of pride. **Proverbs 16:18, 19** teaches about the pitfall of pride: ***"Pride goes before destruction, a haughty spirit before a fall. Better to be lowly in spirit along with the oppressed than to share plunder with the proud."*** What exactly do these verses mean?

A prideful attitude does nothing to build others up or to edify. Just the opposite is true. Pride keeps people from humbling themselves before God and realizing their need for salvation. It separates us from God. We don't experience that genuine relationship with Him that He so desires.

Pride in children keeps parents from seeing their children's faults and from disciplining and correcting them to make them better. Pride in self keeps us selfish and self-centered. Only God knows how many nations, marriages, families, churches, businesses, lives, etc. have been wrecked by pride. Nevertheless, it's our choice whether we allow pride to be in control.

Jesus' example is the one we should follow. Consider **Philippians 2:5-7**:

Have the same mindset as Christ Jesus: Who, being in very nature God, did not consider equality with God something to be used to his own advantage; rather, he made himself nothing by taking the very nature of a servant, being made in human likeness.

Put away selfish pride and drink the Joy Juice of Jesus with a humble attitude.

Prayer: *I come to You today, Lord, as humbly as I know how. You have blessed me beyond description, and I thank You for each and every one of those* *blessings that You have poured out into my life. It is my tendency sometimes to take credit for some of the good things that bring me such joy, but as I focus totally on You, I am reminded that everything is a gift from my loving, generous, Heavenly Father. Give me Your attitude so that I will exemplify You in all that I do today and everyday.*

Abundant Joy Juice

Have you had your Joy Juice today? Don't let pride get in the way; drink it regardless of who's watching.

Peer pressure is always a challenge. From youngsters to seniors, the influence is always there. The Bible never uses the phrase "peer pressure," but it does tell us how we should face the many trials that will come our way, and these trials frequently include pressure from our peers. **Romans 12:2** exhorts us: *"Do not conform to the pattern of this world, but be transformed by the renewing of your mind. Then you will be able to test and approve what God's will is—his good, pleasing and perfect will."*

Often when people succumb to peer pressure, it's because they allow pride to take hold and rule their thinking. They don't want to appear different or "uncool". They want to fit in with the crowd. In other words, their thinking has conformed to *"the pattern of this world."* But when we completely sell out to God and are faithful in our prayer time and Bible reading, we will be changed and *"transformed*

by the renewing of our mind." That's when we will experience a boldness to stand up for our convictions.

No matter what your age, at times you will feel the pressures of the world pulling at you. Let's get into the habit of never making a choice without first consulting Jesus. He always has the answer and will help us to stand up to peer pressure. If we are living according to his "***good, pleasing and perfect will***," then we'll be drinking much more Joy Juice than when we conform to the enticements of the world.

Speaking of peer pressure and pride, offer the joy of the Lord to your friends and watch the transformations begin.

Prayer: *Help me to take a close look at my own heart today, Lord. Am I afraid of what others think? Am I ashamed to stand boldly for You? I desire to be totally transformed into Your likeness, and that means standing against certain things which will* *make me appear different. Please fill me with Your courage, wisdom, and strength to do what is pleasing in Your sight and to do Your perfect will. I desire for You to be proud of me—in the good sense of the word.*

Abundant Joy Juice

Have you had your Joy Juice today? If you are drinking it faithfully, you'll find yourself on the road to overcoming pride.

We know that we all have a sin problem—and one of those sins is pride. We will not overcome this pride issue until we understand the sinfulness of it. Pastor Joe Thorn points out that many people underestimate the danger of pride:

[Many] *tend to treat the sin of pride like a neighborhood dog. We know it can bite us, but for some reason we don't think it will. The truth is, it will devour us. Until we understand the danger of this sin, and begin taking it seriously, we will never overcome it.* [2]

One suggestion to help us overcome the pride issue in our lives is to surround ourselves with humble, Christian men and women. Instead of seeking the company of those who value material wealth, possessions, social status, or power, we need to align ourselves with those who exhibit humility and godliness. Find people who look like Christ, who have the attitude of Jesus (humility and servitude).

As we read and study the Holy Bible, we find a variety of men and women who learned the hard way to be humble. Some never learned, and pride was their downfall. One of my favorite examples of learning humility is Paul. He came to understand his need for that *"thorn in the flesh"* that God sent to keep him humble (**2 Cor. 12:7, KJV**). And he could proclaim, *"Christ Jesus came into the world to save sinners—***of whom I am the worst"* (**1 Tim 1:15**).

Turn that serving of Joy Juice up to your lips today, and begin to joyfully thank God for the thorns which keep you humble.

Prayer: *Thorns hurt, dear Jesus. And I don't like them. But You haven't asked me to like them, have You? You've only asked me to praise You in spite of* *them and to trust You to know what is best for me. Use those thorns to humble me in my prideful areas of life and help me to be a godly example of humility. Make my heart as tender as Paul's.*

Abundant Joy Juice

Have you had your Joy Juice today? Let's go green and drink it naturally.

There's a lot of talk lately about "going green." When most people use this term, they are referring to the many different ways you can choose to take care of our environment—things like carpooling, saving energy, recycling, etc.

I'd like for us to think about another type of "green" today. It's the big green *J,* and I'm not referring to joy. As a matter of fact, this *J* steals your joy. It's the feeling you get when someone else has something that you want. It's the emotion that wells up inside when another person gets recognized on the job, yet you *know* you've done a better job. We all experience it from time to time. It's the green-eyed monster called jealousy.

Galatians 5:19 lists jealousy among the acts of the sinful nature that will keep us from inheriting the kingdom of God. Just a tiny bit of jealousy taking root in our hearts can lead to bitterness, resentment, anger, rudeness, a critical spirit, and eventually loss of relationship.

What is the cure? Since jealousy begins in the mind, let's turn to **Philippians 4: 8, 9** to find the antidote for our jealous thoughts:

Finally, brothers and sisters, whatever is true, whatever is noble, whatever is right, whatever is pure, whatever is lovely, whatever is admirable—if anything is excellent or praiseworthy—think about such things.

Though we all would like a healthier environment, I'm asking you *not* to "go green" if it includes being jealous. Instead, let's set our minds on what is excellent and praiseworthy and thus experience peace and joy

Prayer: *Jealousy sneaks up on me sometimes, Lord. I ask that You put a hedge of protection around*

my heart so that I will not let it seep in and catch me unaware. Give me Your love for my fellow colleagues, friends, and family members so that I will not react with jealousy, though the normal tendency is to do so. Take away my critical spirit and replace it with a joyful one.

Abundant Joy Juice

Have you had your Joy Juice today? Think of others, and share some with them. It always helps when we put others before ourselves.

Do you have a humble spirit or a jealous one? If your thoughts are focused on Christ, you begin to see things as He would see them, and your attitude is one of humility and joy. But, if our eyes are on ourselves, what happens? We begin to envy others because we don't have everything they do. We completely forget how blessed we are in other areas. All we see is what we *don't* have.

Jealousy! As I wrote down the word and looked at it closely, the last five letters jumped out at me: L-O-U-S-Y. That spells *lousy*. How appropriate, because that's exactly how it makes us feel. Wouldn't you agree? Maybe we should be pronouncing it that way. Instead of saying *jealousy*, let's read it *jea-lousy* to be reminded that when our hearts are full of envy, GEE, it makes us feel LOUSY!

Let's go to **Colossians 3:12-15** to find weapons to combat this "enemy:"

Therefore, as God's chosen people, holy and dearly loved, clothe yourselves with compassion, kindness, humility, gentleness and patience. Bear with each other and forgive one another if any of you has a grievance against someone. Forgive as the Lord forgave you. And over all these virtues put on love, which binds them all together in perfect unity.

Now, I don't know about you, but I don't like feeling lousy. So I'm choosing to clothe myself in the above mentioned attire and constantly sip my Joy Juice. Wanna join me?

Prayer: *Gee, Lord! Protect me from that ole ugly enemy of jealousy. It seems to hide behind every opportunity and is around each corner. May I be reminded to put on my glasses which give me spiri-*

tual clarity. When I see anything with even a hint of "green" in my life, give me the wisdom to know how to get rid of it. Give me a forgiving heart, reminding me that You have forgiven me. I choose to put on love and enjoy the spirit of unity.

Have you had your Joy Juice today? It will help to combat that debilitating disease called jealousy.

Just as we pick up germs and bacteria that cause illnesses, we also are attacked by influences that cause the undesirable result of jealousy. To battle this disease, let's think about the root causes. Jealousy typically grows out of insecurity, fear, deception, or the coveting of what someone else has. The Bible addresses each of these root causes several times.

Often we base our personal security on the opinion, affirmation, and acceptance of other people. When we feel rejected or unloved, we become dangerously insecure, leading us to perceive other people as threats to our own well being. To battle insecurity, we must turn to God through His Word to tell us repeatedly of His unfailing love and acceptance. We know He loves us, but often we need to be reminded by opening our Bible and reading passages affirming that love:

- ***But I trust in your unfailing love; my heart rejoices in your salvation. I will sing the***

LORD's praise, for he has been good to me. **(Ps. 13:5,6)**
- *Let the morning bring me word of your unfailing love, for I have put my trust in you. Show me the way I should go, for to you I entrust my life.* **(Ps. 143:8)**
- *I love those who love me, and those who seek me find me.* **(Prov. 8:17)**

Now, don't you already feel better? Take a big swallow of Joy Juice and feel God's love wash all the jealousy away.

Prayer: *All my life I've been taught that God is love. If I truly believe that, Lord, I should be expecting and accepting Your love daily. So, I do make a conscious effort to experience Your love as I ask You to take control of my life. Shine Your light on the sin of jealousy, and wash it away as I drink in Your joy.*

Have you had your Joy Juice today? Never fear; a healthy remedy is here.

We've discussed on the previous pages how personal insecurity can breed symptoms of jealousy. Fear can be another instigator. A life of fear is just as devastating to relationships as insecurity. Controlling through fear will not help you maintain the relationships or positions you desire. It has been said that there is nothing we can hang on to that is worth what we are giving up. This statement refers to the peace we can know through Jesus Christ when we give Him free reign over our lives. In the end, jealousy does not keep, it pushes away.

To overcome fear, we need to first recognize what we fear, confess it before God, and then transform our thoughts through God's Word. **1 John 4:18** speaks of fear: *"There is no fear in love. But perfect love drives out fear, because fear has to do with punishment. The one who fears is not made perfect in love."*

John is reminding us of the love of Christ. We can resolve our fears by focusing on his immeasurable love for us and then by allowing Him to love others through us. His love will quiet our fears and give us confidence. *God*-confidence, that is! Not self-confidence.

So, as **Jude 24** so beautifully proclaims, let's dedicate our life ***"to him who is able to keep you from stumbling and to present you before his glorious presence without fault and with great joy."*** Soak in the love of Christ so that you are filled to overflowing. No more room for jealously—but lots of room for joy.

Prayer: *Drive out all fear, Father God, by saturating me with Your love. As soon as that first fearful thought tries to take root in my mind, bring to my remembrance how much You love me and that You will protect me. There is no need to fear because You are always near. Oh, what joy that brings to my heart!*

Have you had your Joy Juice today? Don't let anyone deceive you into thinking you shouldn't drink it continually and consistently.

Did you realize that deception can play a role in cultivating jealousy in your heart? Many people perceive a threat that, in reality, does not exist. Their perception of life is distorted due to lies they believe about others and themselves.

All of us would be stronger spiritually if we would consistently meditate on scriptures such as **John 8:32**: *"Then you will know the truth, and the truth will set you free."* And then **John 16:13:** *"But when he, the Spirit of truth, comes, he will guide you into all the truth."* Let's not let the enemy deceive us and draw us into jealousy. That deception destroys relationships and does *not* bring joy.

Another cause of jealousy is coveting what others possess. This leads to aggressive jealousy that is often spoken against in the Bible. The Ten Commandments address the issue: *"You shall not covet your neighbor's house. You shall not covet your neighbor's wife, or his male or female servant, his ox or donkey, or anything that belongs to your neighbor"* (**Ex. 20:17**).

We covet when we are not satisfied with the blessings God has given us. We should pray for a grateful heart. That means opening our thankful eyes to all we do have.

No matter what the cause of jealousy—whether it be insecurity, fear, deception, or covetousness—the key to overcoming this disease is to discern the roots of your jealousy and then battle them with the truth of God's Word. Let's join one another in asking the Lord to let us *"be transformed by the renewing of [our] mind[s]"* (**Rom. 12:2**).

Prayer: *Father, I do not want to be a jealous person. Unroot any insecurity, fear, deception, or traces of covetousness that may be trying to grow in my heart. May I pant after You and be so thirsty for Your Word* *that my mind and my life is transformed to be more like You with each passing day. My desire is to be a joy to You, Lord. And that will bring joy to my heart.*

Chapter Eleven

✺

Tunes and Tales
Of
Joy Juice

�֎

Have you had your Joy Juice today? This is the perfect day to enjoy it—

especially if you're feeling a little gloomy.

Have you noticed how some folks seem to make up their minds to enjoy their misery? And they want to sing about it all day long! That reminds me of the silly song written by Buck Owens and Roy Clark for the TV classic *Hee Haw*. I chuckle every time I think back to the group who would sing this tune:

Gloom, despair, and agony on me.
Deep, dark depression, excessive misery.
If it weren't for bad luck, I'd have no luck at all
Gloom, despair, and agony on me! [1]

Abundant Joy Juice

Aren't we glad that we can choose joy instead of misery, gloom, and despair? Let's not become the kind of person whom everyone dreads to see coming because of the sad tale of despair that will be sung. Even in the midst of trying, difficult times, we still have a choice regarding how we will react to those circumstances.

There are many times we could choose to focus on the economy, politics, the unpredictable weather, and many "What ifs" which cause us to fret. Instead, why don't we follow the instruction of the psalmist who wrote, ***"The LORD has done it this very day; let us rejoice today and be glad"*** **(Ps. 118:24)**?

Do you wake up each morning with a song of praise in your heart? It's our choice, you know. We should look forward expectantly to each new day. Anticipate joyful things—not gloom and despair. As one of my friends wisely said, "No matter what happens, if we have God by our side, we will have joy."

So, come on! Let's *choose* to rejoice in this new day that the Lord has given us. Pack your picnic basket full of Joy Juice, and set about enjoying this journey called life.

Prayer: *Precious Savior, who died that I might have an abundant life of joy, please constantly remind me that I always have a choice to wallow in my pity and circumstances or to rise above them by focusing on You. Each new day is a gift, and I rejoice in this day by having a song of joy in my heart. It's a heart-song about You, my loving Father, who is always near.*

Have you had your Joy Juice today? As you drink it, you may feel your heart filling up with joy.

So often I'm reminded of my daddy singing at the top of his lungs, proclaiming his faith in God. He was the song leader in his country church, but he didn't sing *only* in church. He sang around the house, in the car, while he was working, and while at play. He was full of the joy of the Lord, and he couldn't help singing about it.

I'm pretty sure this is what the scripture means in **Deuteronomy 11:18,19**:

Fix these words of mine in your hearts and minds; tie them as symbols on your hands and bind them on your foreheads. Teach them to your children, talking about them when you sit at home and when you walk along the road, when you lie down and when you get up.

In the last few years, I've come to really appreciate what Daddy taught me simply by allowing his Joy Juice to overflow into my life. We can all choose to let the sunshine of Jesus brighten our day. Consider the lyrics to "Sunshine in My Soul:"

There is sunshine in my soul today,
More glorious and bright
Than glows in any earthly sky,
For Jesus is my light.
O there's sunshine, blessed sunshine,
While the peaceful, happy moments roll;
When Jesus shows His smiling face
There is sunshine in my soul.
There is gladness in my soul today,
And hope, and praise, and love,
For blessings which He gives me now,
For joys laid up above. [2]

When people look at your life, do they see joy overflowing from you? Is your Joy Juice jug spilling out onto your children, grandchildren, and the young people who are being influenced by your example? Only you and God can answer that question truthfully. Go before Him today, and get an honest answer.

Prayer: *Fill my heart and soul with Your sunshine, Your joy, Your gladness. Make me a joyful blessing to all those around me, especially the children who will one day think back over the time we spent together. May they have special memories of the song of joy that is the theme of my life because of my relationship with You, precious Lord.*

Have you had your Joy Juice today? When you're faithfully drinking in the joy of the Lord every day of your life, you will become a channel of blessing to others.

I love the praise and worship music that is sung in our churches today. It is a great avenue of communing with God and helps me enter into worship. But let's not forget the richness of the hymns of old. For example, the lyrics of the beautiful hymn "Make Me a Channel of Blessing" hold such truth:

Is your life a channel of blessing?
Is the love of God flowing through you?
Are you telling the lost of the Savior?
Are you ready His service to do?

Is your life a channel of blessing?
Are you burdened for those that are lost?
Have you urged upon those who are straying,
The Savior Who died on the cross?

Is your life a channel of blessing?
Is it a daily telling for Him?
Have you spoken the Word of salvation
To those who are dying in sin?

We cannot be channels of blessing
If our lives are not free from known sin;
We will barriers be and a hindrance
To those we are trying to win.

Chorus:
Make me a channel of blessing today,
Make me a channel of blessing, I pray;
My life possessing, my service blessing,
Make me a channel of blessing today. [3]

May we each be a channel of blessing, avenues that lead others to Christ. May our lives be so filled with His truth, His peace, and His joy that others will be drawn to a saving knowledge of Jesus as

Abundant Joy Juice

their Savior. Serve others a huge helping of Joy Juice today.

Prayer: *Go back to the words of this song and make it your prayer today.*

Abundant Joy Juice

Have you had your Joy Juice today? Store up plenty so that you'll always have lots to share for every season.

Many of you know that I'm a country gal. We country girls learned from our moms all about putting up vegetables and fruits for the winter. My parents always had a summer garden. There was no choice for us kids—the whole family helped to pick, gather, and prepare food, anticipating the seasons when there would be no fresh produce.

As a good farmer's daughter should, I still do a little of that from time to time. Not long ago, I was putting fresh vegetables in our freezer when the story of "The Little Red Hen" came floating out my memory bank and into the forefront of my mind. Do you remember the story? It goes something like this: The Little Red Hen finds a grain of wheat and asks for help from the other farm animals to plant it. But none of the animals will volunteer to help her. At each stage of the preparation—harvest, threshing, milling the wheat into flour, and even the baking of the bread—the hen continues to ask for help from her friends. She gets no assistance whatsoever.

Finally, all the hard work is done, and it's time to eat the bread. At this time, all the animals want to volunteer to help with the tasting. However, she declines their "help" at this point, stating that no one helped with the preparation and hard work, so she and her chicks would simple finish the task themselves. The moral of the story is that those who aren't willing to help shouldn't expect to enjoy the end product. [4]

I'm happy to report that I usually have help with my gardening projects. But the story of "The Little Red Hen" reminds me of the verse in **2 Thessalonians 3:10** where we read, *"the one who is unwilling to work shall not eat."*

We know that some people are not able to work. But if God has given us the strength and ability, we should willingly help others and ourselves. We should always be willing to share Christ's love in an attitude of service. Let's be extra diligent in sharing the joy of the Lord by offering our help when we see a need. A side benefit is that hard work brings joyful satisfaction when the job is completed.

Prayer: *Heavenly Father, thank You for the strength and health that You have given me to be able to work. May I never be lazy and slothful but always be willing to work hard to provide for my family, as well as help others along the way. Give me eyes to see needs that may otherwise go unnoticed, and fill me with compassion, ability, and fortitude to get the tasks done.*

Abundant Joy Juice

Have you had your Joy Juice today? It's really good for you. That's the truth!

Do you know folks who always jump to conclusions? And, of course, many times, it's the wrong conclusion. I guess we're all guilty from time to time. It's kind of like the fable entitled "Henny Penny" (or "Chicken Little).

For those of you too young to remember the story or for those who have forgotten, the gist of the tale goes like this: Henny Penny is eating her lunch one day and an acorn falls on her head. She jumps to the conclusion that the sky is falling. Immediately, she sets out to tell the king. On her journey, she meets other animals who join her in the quest: Turkey Lurkey, Ducky Luckey, Goosey Loosey, and a host of others. Finally, they meet Foxy Loxy, who offers the hen and her friends his help to find their way to the king. Of course, he is cunning and is trying to entrap them so that he can eat them for dinner. [5]

All of us need to be aware of the "Foxy Loxys" of life. This character is called by several names in the Bible, such as enemy, devil, Satan, and deceiver. **1 Peter 5:8** warns us: *"Be alert and of sober mind . Your enemy the devil prowls around like a roaring lion looking for someone to devour."*

What lessons can we draw from the fable "Henny Penny"?

1. Don't jump to conclusions.
2. Don't spread untruth.
3. Don't fall for the enemy's cunning plots.

Stay clear minded and alert; speak only what you know to be truth, and drink the Joy Juice of Jesus so that you will be aware of the enemy's plots.

Prayer: *Father, You've warned us to be on the alert. Help me to see the enemy's schemes for just what they are—plots to keep me from drawing closer to You. Please show me Your perfect plan for my life, and give me the wisdom to take one step at time, holding Your hand as I go.*

Abundant Joy Juice

Have you had your Joy Juice today? It'll keep you from huffing and puffing along the way throughout your day.

We all remember the fairy tale of "The Three Little Pigs," right? It came time for the pigs to leave home and seek their fortunes. Before they left, their mother told them something like, "Whatever you do, do it to the best of your ability, because that's the way to get ahead in the world."

The first little pig didn't listen; he built his house out of straw because it was the easiest thing to do. The second little pig built his house out of sticks. This was a little bit stronger than a straw house, but the third little pig fared the best by building his house out of bricks. He made a wise choice by following his mom's advice.

You know what happened next! Along came the big, bad wolf. He huffed and puffed, trying to blow the houses down. The first and second little pigs lost their homes because they'd not built them out of the best materials. The only house left standing after all that huffing and puffing was the house made of bricks. The wise little pig had listened to his mother and had built the very best house he could out of the strongest materials he could find. His house was built on a firm foundation. [6]

Is your spiritual house built on the firm foundation of Jesus Christ? If so, no matter what wolves come into your life, they can huff and puff and puff and huff, but they'll never be able to blow your faith away, for **"God is [your] refuge and strength, an ever-present help in trouble" (Ps. 46:1).**

Let's take a lesson from the third little pig and build a strong faith in God so that we will withstand the wolves who often strive to blow away our joy and faith.

Prayer: *How often I feel under attack from the forces which seem to be like devouring wolves. But, Father, I know You are always there, always stronger, always* *in control, guarding my "house." Thank You for your ever-present love and protection. Keep me from doubting Your willingness and ability to look after me in all circumstances. I face today with a calm, joyful assurance.*

Abundant Joy Juice

Have you had your Joy Juice? Be grateful for what you have, and enjoy your special serving as you drink it today.

It's human nature to always want something that we don't have. From the beginning of time in the Garden of Eden up until today, we humans have made poor choices because we are not content with what God has given us.

Even Aesop's fable "The Goose that Laid the Golden Eggs," which first originated in the 6th century BC, points out this truth. The story goes something like this:

A cottager and his wife had a Hen that laid a golden egg every day. They supposed that the Hen must contain a great lump of gold in its inside, and in order to get the gold they killed it. Having done so, they found to their surprise that the Hen differed in no respect from their other hens. The foolish pair, thus hoping to become rich all at once, deprived themselves of the gain of which they were assured day by day.[7]

In **Philippians 4:11** Paul teaches, ***"For I have learned to be content whatever the circumstances."*** Would you say that you are content? When our thoughts are always on material things or on those things that we don't have, then we are not going to be satisfied. We'll just find ourselves wanting more, more, more. But when we allow God to fill us, then we will learn to be content because all we really need is Him. **1 Timothy 6:6** says it well: ***"But godliness with contentment is great gain."***

Drink that Joy Juice faithfully, and be content with the flavor God gives you today.

Prayer: *Contentment in You, Lord, that's what I desire. Fill me up with Your love, Your joy, Your truth. I desire to overflow with the golden principles* *taught in Your Word. May I bring You joy, Father, as I become more and more content with simply being Yours.*

Abundant Joy Juice

Have you had your Joy Juice today? Don't let your pitcher get so low that you have a hard time pouring yourself a nice serving.

As you fly through this busy day, be reminded of Aesop's fable "The Crow and the Pitcher." Here's the story:

A crow, half-dead with thirst, came upon a pitcher which had once been full of water; but when the crow put its beak into the mouth of the pitcher, he found that only very little water was left in it, and that he could not reach far enough down to get at it. He tried, and he tried, but at last had to give up in despair.

Then a thought came to him, and he took a pebble and dropped it into the pitcher. Then he took another pebble and dropped it into the pitcher. Then he took another pebble and dropped that into the pitcher. Then he took another pebble and dropped that into

the pitcher. At last, at last, he saw the water mount up near him, and after casting in a few more pebbles, he was able to quench his thirst and save his life.
Little by little does the trick. [8]

Are you facing a task or a circumstance that seems impossible? Don't give up hope! Ask the Lord to help you, to give you wisdom, a new perspective, and the perseverance to keep pushing forward. In **Philippians 3:14** Paul tells us to persevere: ***"I press on toward the goal to win the prize for which God has called me heavenward in Christ Jesus."***

So instead of flitting and flopping around, flying aimlessly, and fretting over our situations, let's pick up those pebbles of wisdom gained by reading God's Word and listen to His voice as He directs us to the pitcher filled with Joy Juice. Press on toward the joyful goal of eternity with Christ.

Prayer: *Sometimes it seems that the task ahead of me is impossible. But, Lord, I know from studying Your Word and from simply observing Your faithfulness through the years that* nothing *is impossible with You. Give me new ways of approaching the problems life seems to serve up, and give me the fortitude to stand strong until You teach me what I need to know. I thank You for never giving up on me.*

Abundant Joy Juice

Have you had your Joy Juice today? Nothing can take the place of authentic joy that comes from knowing you are loved.

Do you *know* that you can count on the promises of God? The Bible is God's inerrant word; many times throughout the pages of this sacred book, we are told that God is love. He loved us so much that He sent His Son to die for us.

Some days we tend to believe in God's love more than other days. When things are going well and we don't have any major problems, we might believe that God really and truly loves us. But what about when the rug is jerked out from under us? What about the times we're hurt by circumstances that God has allowed into our lives? Do we *feel* loved then?

Writer Grantley Morris says, "Scripture makes no promise that you will always feel loved, nor that circumstances will always make it obvious that you are loved. God simply promises that you are loved. No suffering or tragedy will ever separate you from God's love (**Rom. 8:35-39**). A snap-shot in time proves nothing. Only eternity's movies can adequately portray the infinitude of God's love for you." [9]

Let's look at those reassuring words of **Romans 8:38, 39**:

For I am convinced that neither death nor life, neither angels nor demons, neither the present nor the future, nor any powers, neither height nor depth, nor anything else in all creation, will be able to separate us from the love of God that is in Christ Jesus our Lord.

You are loved—even though some days you may forget to drink your Joy Juice.

Prayer: *Loving Father, thank You for loving me, even when I am so unlovable. For those many times when*

You forgive my shortcomings and smile at my mistakes, knowing that's how I learn to be more Christ-like, I praise Your name. I am extremely grateful for the truth that nothing can separate me from Your love. What a joyful comfort!

Abundant Joy Juice

Have you had your Joy Juice today? God made some especially for you just because you have a special place in His heart. Sing a tune or recall a tale of joy, and share it with your loved ones today.

Many of you are probably like me and have wonderful memories of grandparents. My grandmother would let me get in the kitchen with her to make my own "baby biscuits" as she cooked up the real deal. She'd play with me and let me "help" her with jobs that I'm sure she could have done much more quickly without me. She would tell me stories and teach me songs. I can remember laughing lots of good belly laughs with Grandma. My memories of her are filled with joy.

As a child, I didn't understand the depth of her love—even though I loved her with all my heart. Now, however, in this season of life, I truly understand and appreciate her patient, unconditional love. The reason I can understand it now is that I am a grandmother myself. I so enjoy letting my precious bundles of joy help me with little chores around the house. No, they don't do things perfectly—far from it. Sometimes their "help" causes this "GiGi," as they call me, to have more work cleaning up the mess we've made. But the mess doesn't matter because I would much rather see their smiles of delight and the enjoyment of simply being together. Their joy brings me joy because they have a special place in my heart.

Oh, the pleasure of teaching them songs and telling them stories. Sometimes it's the same story over and over again, but the smiles on their faces make it all worthwhile. We have one "knock-knock" joke that we've told each other umpteen hundred times, and we laugh uncontrollably every time. Now, that's the joy of grandchildren!

Don't you think that's how it is with God? He doesn't really need our help, but He enjoys seeing our joy as we help Him. We have a special place in God's heart, and He invites us to be a part of His will and His joy. He loves us unconditionally. He receives joy from seeing us enjoy being His.

Prayer: *Father, thank You for sharing Your joy with me. Thank You for loving me so much that You allow me to be a part of Your work and Your plan. Show me how to spread Your love and joy with all the people You bring into my life, both young and old. Knock-Knock! Who's there? God's love and joy—everywhere!*

This devotional is dedicated to Nathan, Naomi, Will, Jude, Samuel and Sara...and any other grand-joys to come!

Chapter Twelve

✳

Joy Juice
Droplets of Prayer and Grace

Have you had your Joy Juice today? Sit quietly as you drink in the joy of Jesus during your prayer time.

Prayer is such an important part of developing a relationship with God. Over and over again in His Word, He exhorts us to pray. What are we to pray about? Everything! Now, I can hear some of you saying, "But, some things are not important enough to bother God. He has more urgent things to think about than something as insignificant as my small problem."

Well, let me tell you something, friend. If it's important to you, it's important to God. Nothing is too small or too big to bring to the Father in prayer.

Philippians 4:6 urges us to pray about matters minor and urgent: *"Don't worry about anything; instead, pray about everything. Tell God what you need, and thank him for all he has done"* (**NLT**).

Do I need to repeat the part of the verse that says *"pray about everything"*? Pray about:

- Your family
- Your relationships
- Your job
- Your spiritual growth
- Your major and minor decisions
- Your problems—large or small

And may I suggest that we pray for God to use us as His instruments to deliver the joy of the Lord into the hearts of those we meet today and every day? Let's ask God for an extra measure of joy to share with others along our way.

Prayer: *Prayer time is such a special time, Lord. Help me to see it as such a privilege and honor to come before You with everything. May I always trust You with every detail of my life. From this time forward, help me to rely on You 100 percent of the time, knowing that Your plan already includes the details of my journey through life.*

Have you had your Joy Juice today? I pray that you have; and I hope that you received a joyful answer to your prayer as you prayed with joy.

When God answers our prayer with a "no" or a "not now", why do we assume that He has not answered our prayer at all? Do we truly trust Him to do what is best for us, or do we selfishly want our own way? Many times we pray, asking for something that we perceive as a *need* in our life. But God, in His infinite wisdom, knows that it is not what we need at all; it's simply our *want*.

Ephesians 3:20 tells us of His power to answer: *"Now to him who is able to do immeasurably more than all we ask or imagine, according to his power that is at work within us."* If we will allow Him to take complete control of our lives and pray faithfully for His will, then through His power, He will do immeasurably more (exceedingly, abundantly more) than all we ask or imagine.

Dr. Wayne Barber explains it well:

When does God move in and do those things that are exceeding abundantly beyond what we ask or think? When the Holy Spirit has empowered us, when Christ has indwelt us, when His love has mastered us and when His fullness has filled us. [1]

As we pray each day, throughout the day, along our way, may we be so in love with Jesus that we accept the no and not now answers just as joyfully as we do the yes answers to our prayers.

Prayer: *Dear Lord, You are the God of wisdom and power. Help me to trust in Your timing and Your answers to my prayers. May I learn to praise You—regardless of how You answer my prayer requests. Each answer is an expression of Your love for me, and that is a reason to be joyful in all things.*

Have you had your Joy Juice today? Sometimes we have to humble ourselves before we can savor the delicious taste. Consider **2 Chronicles 7:14**:

"If my people, who are called by my name, will humble themselves and pray and seek my face and turn from their wicked ways, then I will hear from heaven, and I will forgive their sin and will heal their land."

Do you think our land needs healing? We don't have to look far to see that people throughout our country are suffering in countless ways. From natural disasters to disasters of our own making, people all across America are hurting.

Let's go back to that verse again in **2 Chronicles** and apply it to our nation. It says, *"If my people,"* and *if* is an important word. *If we will:*

1. Humble ourselves
2. Pray

3. Seek God's face
4. Turn from our wicked ways

Then He will hear us, forgive our sin, and will heal our land. God is willing to do His part, but we must do our part. We partner with him, not out of obligation, but out of love for Him, others, and for our country.

Let's humble ourselves before God in prayer, seek His face, ask for forgiveness, and then wait expectantly for Him to heal our land. May the joy of the Lord be our strength (**Neh. 8:10**).

Prayer: *So often, Father, I just hastily throw my prayers Your way without even stopping to recognize Your goodness, graciousness, faithfulness, and majesty. May I always be aware that it should be with humility and a genuine heart of love that I come before You. I pray for our country; our land needs healing. Show us our wicked ways, and then give us the courage, fortitude, and desire to turn from those ways which pull us far from You.*

Have you had your Joy Juice today? It's created with pure ingredients and is sure to help you have a prayerful heart.

Many of us see the need for prayerful intercession for our country. A while ago, Dr. Charles Stanley led a challenge for Christians in America to commit to praying for twenty weeks (140 days) about a variety of issues facing our country. Many of those who fulfilled their commitment began a life-long habit of praying daily for the needs and conditions in our country. Isn't that what we all should be doing? Lifting our country up in prayer should happen 365 days of each year. [2]

Dr. Stanley suggested that we begin our prayer commitment by reading **Psalm 51** in personal preparation. This psalm was written by David and is a plea for mercy, forgiveness, and cleansing. David realized that his heart needed to be right with God, and the words of this psalm indicate a broken, repentant heart, acknowledging the sin in his life.

Listen to David's words in **verses 10-12:**

Create in me a pure heart, O God, and renew a steadfast spirit within me. Do not cast me from your presence or take your Holy Spirit from me. Restore to me the joy of your salvation and grant me a willing spirit, to sustain me.

Like David, we should be on our knees before God, asking for a pure heart. Twice in this short psalm, David asked for the joy he had lost due to his indulgent sin. That's so indicative of what's happening in our country.

May we join together, asking God to give us pure, repentant hearts and a personal, joyful renewal.

Prayer: *A pure heart, Lord. That is my desire. May I genuinely want Your will for me and for my country.*

We live in the best country in the world, founded on Christian principles. Yet, we have strayed. Draw us back to You by creating pure hearts in us; renew our steadfastness, we pray.

Have you had your Joy Juice today? Remember God's faithfulness as you drink in His joy this morning. Then pray with a fervent heart, trusting in His power.

Why is it that we often forget what God has done for us in the past? We find ourselves in a new trial, and we begin to worry and fret, forgetting how He has been real to us before. Maybe we get caught up in the present circumstances and become focused on how we can solve the problem ourselves. Instead, we should immediately recall the faithfulness of God.

Psalm 77 is a beautiful psalm in which the writer eloquently expresses that we can find God's comfort through the difficulties of life. The psalmist remembers how He has helped faithfully in the past. When we get discouraged and feel like giving up, we should recall the miracles and previous unexpected blessings that God has poured out on us. These memories will give us the joyful courage to continue.

In **Psalm 77:13, 14** we read, *"Your ways, God, are holy. What god is as great as our God? You are*

the God who performs miracles; you display your power among the peoples."

God's power is what we should depend on—not our own resources. God is capable of handling whatever comes our way. He is trustworthy. Thank Him in the midst of the trial for His power, His protection, and His love. You might just find that your heart does an about-face and goes from anxiety to peaceful joy.

Prayer: *"Your ways, God, are holy. What god is as great as our God? You are the God who performs miracles; you display your power among the peoples." May* **Psalm 77: 13, 14** *be my prayer today and in the days to come as I need to focus on the power of You, my loving God.*

Abundant Joy Juice

Have you had your Joy Juice today? When you're full of joy, you'll be more aware of God's grace.

Grace. We hear the word used often. Sometimes it's used as a girl's name. (My sweet niece is Amanda Grace.) At mealtime, we say "grace" by asking God's blessing on our food. When someone moves with poise and confidence, we say they are "graceful." But what do we mean when we talk about God's grace?

It must be important because grace is mentioned 170 times in the Bible. Simply put, grace is God's unmerited favor; it is God doing good for us, even though we are not good. God's grace offers us eternal life and a promise of heaven, though we do not deserve these gifts. We can have God's grace because of the sacrifice of our Lord Jesus Christ.

Lysa Terkeurst writes the following about this mysterious and wonderful word:

Grace doesn't give me a free pass to act out how I feel, with no regard to His commands. Rather His grace gives me consolation in the moment, with a challenge to learn from this situation and become more mature in the future. Grace is the sugar that helps the bitter pills of confession and repentance to go down without choking. That's why the writer of Hebrews says, **'Let us then approach the throne of grace with confidence, so that we may receive mercy and find grace to help us in our time of need'** **(Heb. 4:16).** *[3]*

God's grace and joy go hand in hand. Share both with others today.

Prayer: *Father, without Your grace there is no way to have a personal relationship with You. I am so thankful that You have offered me Your unmerited favor, and I gratefully accept this gift. Thank you for bringing Your Son to earth to die for me. May I always know that I can approach the throne of grace with confidence.*

Abundant Joy Juice

Have you had your Joy Juice today? And are you drinking it gracefully?

In one of my quiet times, God led me to a verse that made me think of you: *"Grace and peace be yours in abundance through the knowledge of God and of Jesus our Lord"* (**2 Pet. 1:2**). That's my prayer for you, my friends and readers—that you would experience grace and peace in abundance. Do you want this in your life? It can be yours freely! Look at the verse again. Pay close attention to each word: *"Grace and peace be yours in abundance through the knowledge of God and of Jesus our Lord."*

Many people want an abundance of God's grace and peace, but they are unwilling to put forth the effort to get to know Him better through Bible study and prayer. To enjoy the privileges God offers us, we must seek the knowledge of Him as Peter states in that verse. Just a few minutes a day reading His Word and spending time communicating with Him in prayer will draw you closer to Him. You can't get to know someone if you never spend time with them.

Abundant Joy Juice

The verse speaks of abundant grace and peace. What does that have to do with joy? Everything! They are like fingers on the same hand—the loving hand of God. So open your Bible right now and experience His tender caress on the hurt spots of your heart. Accept His grace so that His peace can take control of your life. This will lead to that joy of the Lord that I'm always talking about.

Though I may not know you personally, you are special to me because you have chosen to read this book. Just know that as the words are being put on this page, I am praying for you. I'm asking God to give you abundant grace and peace, and, of course, the sweet joy that accompanies them.

Prayer: *An abundance of grace, an abundance of peace, and abundance of joy is what I'm requesting, Lord, today. I ask not only for myself, but I ask also for those who you have brought into my life in one* *way or another; please bless each one abundantly. Give us a hunger and thirst to know You better and to bask in the grace that comes from loving and accepting You as our Savior and Lord.*

Have you had your Joy Juice today? It tastes even sweeter when you serve it with grace.

Consider **James 4:6**: *"**But he gives us more grace. That is why Scripture says: 'God opposes the proud but shows favor to the humble.'**"* Grace is God's unmerited favor. It is kindness from God we don't deserve. There is nothing we have done, nor can ever do, to earn this favor. It is a gift from God. My pastor explains grace using this acronym:

God's
Riches
At
Christ's
Expense

In other words, Christ paid with his very life so that we might become heirs of the Kingdom, children of the King. As His children, we inherit the King's riches—like eternal life with Him. Doesn't that make you want to sing with joy?

Grace, grace, God's grace,
Grace that will pardon and cleanse within;
Grace, grace, God's grace,
Grace that is greater than all our sin. [4]

The words of this old hymn say it so perfectly. Won't you accept His forgiveness and grace today? He is the only way to experience a joyful eternity. Now, sing of God's grace because of the abundant joy He has brought to your heart.

Prayer: *God, thank You for Your pardoning grace. Your grace is truly greater than any sin I have ever committed, but help me not to take it for granted or use this truth as an excuse to keep on sinning. Give me strength and wisdom to make good choices and to treat others the way You would have me treat them. Select my words before I open my mouth and control my thoughts and my actions. Gratefully, I accept Your grace with much joy!*

Have you had your Joy Juice today? Drink as much as you'd like. There is no limit to how much you can have.

God's love and grace are limitless. It's hard for our little, finite brains to totally wrap understanding around that concept. God looks at us through eyes of grace. Praise the Lord! He doesn't judge us on our performance. We could never meet His Holy standard, so what a loving blessing He offers us with His grace.

Sarah Young in her book *Jesus Lives* imagines what God would say to us on the subject of grace. Listen as if God were speaking directly to you:

Here is what I see as I view you through eyes of grace: You look regal, for I have clothed you in My royal righteousness. You are radiant, especially when you are gazing at Me. You look lovely as you reflect My Glory back to Me. In fact, you delight Me so much that I rejoice over you with shouts of JOY! Because I am infinite, I can see you simul-

taneously as you are now and as you will be in heaven. The present view helps Me work with you on things you need to change. The heavenly vision enables Me to love you with perfect, everlasting love.[5]

Much of this comes straight from scripture. He covers us in His grace because of his unfailing love for each of us. What an encouragement to know that He doesn't give up on us, but He continues to love us with an everlasting love. Aren't you so thankful for how He loves you? Our hearts should be overflowing with Joy Juice!

Prayer: *Father, indeed, it brings much joy to my heart to think about You rejoicing over me! Help me to remember that only by grace can I be seen as a radiant, regal creature. Thank you for creating me and thank You for the eternity that lies ahead. May I grow more and more like You every day. And may my spiritual growth continually bring joy to You.*

Abundant Joy Juice

Have you had your Joy Juice today? It tastes amazingly good when you are in the center of God's will.

Most all of us recognize the song "Amazing Grace." It's sung in churches all over the world in a variety of languages. Many people choose to use it at funerals and solemn occasions as a source of comfort and strength. But it shouldn't be reserved for sad times. It's a song of hope and praise.

"Amazing Grace" was written by the Englishman John Newton (1725-1807). Once the captain of a slave ship, he converted to Christianity after an encounter with God during a violent storm at sea. He eventually became an ordained minister in the Church of England. The words of this beloved Christian hymn are from a heart of love for the Lord.

Listen to a couple of the verses and see if you can truthfully understand John Newton's heart when he penned the words. If so, you have also experienced God's amazing grace in your life.

Amazing grace, how sweet the sound,
That saved a wretch like me.
I once was lost but now am found,
Was blind, but now I see.
'Twas grace that taught my heart to fear.
And Grace, my fears relieved.
How precious did that Grace appear
The hour I first believed.
When we've been there ten thousand years
Bright shining as the sun.
We've no less days to sing God's praise
Than when we've first begun. [6]

What a glorious time that will be when we can joyfully sing God's praises throughout eternity! Start practicing now so that we can sing together in that heavenly choir. *Amazing grace, how sweet the sound!* Those words bring joy to a sinner like me.

Prayer: *Fill me, dear Heavenly Father, with enough grace to make it through this day. Then give me grace* *tomorrow, the next day, and the next. Remind me that as You extend grace to me daily, I should be willing to do the same for others along the way. Give me the boldness to share Your love, Your grace, and Your joy at every opportunity. My desire is to radiate YOU, both now and throughout eternity.*

Endnotes

✱

Chapter One: A Gulp of Glorified Joy Juice

1. Scott, Clara H., "Open My Eyes, That I May See," *Cyber Hymnal*, http://www.cyberhymnal.org/htm/o/p/openeyes.htm.
2. Kitchens, James A., *Talking to Ducks* (New York: Simon & Schuster, 1994).
3. Southerland, Mary, "Be a Joy Giver," August 14, 2009, *Girlfriends-in-God*, http://www.crosswalk.com/devotionals/girlfriends/girlfriends-in-god-aug-14-2009-11607373.html.
4. Southerland, Mary, "Be a Joy Giver," August 14, 2009, *Girlfriends-in-God*, http://www.cross-

walk.com/devotionals/girlfriends/girlfriends-in-god-aug-14-2009-11607373.html.

5. Patti, Sandi, *Friendship Company CD,* Producers Greg Nelson and Sandi Patti, (1989).

6. Tucker, John, "Improving Your Serve," *The Bible Network*, http://www.bible.net.nz/TUCKER/sermon_20031116.htm.

7. Gaither, William, "Because He Lives" (Gaither Copyright Management, 1971).

Chapter Two:

Generously Give Giant Servings of Joy Juice

1. "One Dollar and 100 Dollar Bill," *Inspirational Christian Stories and Poems*, http://www.inspirationalarchive.com/inspirationalstoriesblog/category/money/.

2. *Life Application Bible NIV* (Wheaton: Tyndale House, 1988, 1989, 1990, 1991), 1049.

3. "The Sacrifice of Joy, Thanksgiving and Praise," *Best Music & Worship Resources,* http://www.rodbest.com/devotional%2016.html.
4. http://www.lifeway.com/lwc/article_main_page/0,1703,A%3D153666&M%3D50018,00.html.
5. Smith, Harper G. (1903), Public Domain.

Chapter Three: Abundant Joy Juice

1. Wilkinson, Bruce, *The Prayer of Jabez Devotional* (Sisters: Multnomah Publishers, Inc., 2001), 7.
2. "ABC's of Evangelism," *New Image Outreach,* http://newimageoutreach.com/abcs-of-evangelism
3. Whittle, Daniel W., "There Shall Be Showers of Blessing," *Cyber Hymnal, http://www.cyberhymnal.org/htm/t/h/thershow.htm.*

Chapter Four: Children Love Joy Juice

1. "Who You Are Speaks Louder to Me Than Anything You Can Say," *Spiritual Endeavors,* http://www.spiritualendeavors.org/inspirational-stories/who-you-are.htm.

2. Rogers, Adrian, *Ten Secrets for a Successful Family* (Wheaton: Crossway Books, 1996), 89-90.

3. McCullough, Mamie, Ph.D., Author, Speaker and Encourager. Dallas, Texas.

4. "God Loves You More Than Anyone," *Talk Jesus,* http://www.talkjesus.com/daily-devotionals/21132-god-loves-you-more-than-anyone.html.

5. "The Little Light of Mine," *Kiddles,* http://www.kiddiles.com/lyrics/t030.html.

6. Warner, Anna and Bradbury, William, "Jesus Loves Me," *All About God,* http://www.all-aboutgod.com/jesus-loves-me.htm.

7. "Deep and Wide," *Child Bible Songs*, http://childbiblesongs.com/song-11-deep-and-wide.shtml.
8. Woolston, Herbert and Root, George F., "Jesus Loves the Little Children," *Kiddles*, http://www.kididdles.com/lyrics/j007.html.
9. "If You're Happy and You Know It," *Kiddles*, http://kiddles.com/lyrics/i007.html.

Chapter Five: Hidden Recipes for Joy Juice

1. http://www.quotegarden.com/live-now.html
2. *Life Application Bible NIV* (Wheaton: Tyndale House, 1988, 1989, 1990, 1991), 1780.
3. "A Cherokee Indian Youth's Rite of Passage (a Legend)," *BigBigForums*, http://www.bigbigforums.com/religion-prayers/548382-cherokee-indian-youths-rite-passage-legend.html.

Chapter Six: Dreaming of Joy Juice

1. McMenamin, Cindi, *When a Woman Discovers Her Dream* (Eugene: Harvest House, 2005), 15.
2. McMenamin, Cindi, *When a Woman Discovers Her Dream* (Eugene: Harvest House, 2005), 19.
3. McMenamin, Cindi, *When a Woman Discovers Her Dream* (Eugene: Harvest House, 2005), 19.
4. McMenamin, Cindi. *When a Woman Discovers Her Dream* (Eugene: Harvest House, 2005), 37-38.
5. *Life Application Bible NIV* (Wheaton: Tyndale House, 1988, 1989, 1990, 1991), 1911.
6. http://www.quotationspage.com/quote/1901.html.

Chapter Seven: Household Uses for Joy Juice

1. Zscheck, Darlene/Hillsong Music, *Jesus, You're All I Need, (c. 1997)*.

Chapter Eight: Garden-grown Joy Juice

1. Life Application Bible NIV (Wheaton: Tyndale House, 1988, 1989, 1990, 1991), 1677.

Chapter Nine: Joy Juice: It's Simply Divine!

1. "A Beautiful Bouquet," *Hamweather*, http://blogs.hamweather.com/2010/04/27/a-beautiful-bouquet/.

Chapter Ten:
Pride and Jealousy: NOT a Recipe for Joy Juice

1. "What Does the Bible Say about Pride?" *gotQuestions.org*, http://www.gotquestions.org/pride-Bible.html.
2. "Overcoming Our Pride," *joethorn.net*, http://www.joethorn.net/2007/09/04/overcoming-our-pride/.

Chapter Eleven: Tunes and Tales of Joy Juice

1. Owens, Buck and Clark, Roy, "Gloom, Despair and Agony on Me", *Hee-Haw (1969-1992)*, *Lyrics Playground*, http://lyricsplayground.com/alpha/songs/g/gloomdespairandagonyonme.shtml.

2. "There Is Sunshine in My Soul Today," *hymnal.net,* http://www.hymnal.net/hymn.php/h/343#ixzz1McJxVOUz.

3. Smyth, Harper Garcia, "Make Me a Channel of Blessing," *Scripture and Music*, http://www.scriptureandmusic.com/Music/Text_Files/Make_Me_A_Channel_Of_Blessing.html.

4. Galdone, Paul, *The Little Red Hen* (New York: Clarion Books, 1973).

5. Galdone, Paul, *Henny Penny* (New York: Clarion Books, 1968).

6. Galdone, Paul, *The Three Little Pigs* (New York: Clarion Books, 1970, 1998).

7. http://en.wikipedia.org/wiki/The_Goose_That_Laid_the_Golden_Eggs#The_story_and_its_moral.

8. "The Crow and the Pitcher," *Aesop's Fables*, http://www.aesopfables.com/cgi/aesop1.cgi?srch&fabl/TheCrowandthePitcher2

9. "God Loves You More Than Anyone," *Talk Jesus*, http://www.talkjesus.com/daily-devotionals/21132-god-loves-you-more-than-anyone.html.

Chapter Twelve:
Joy Juice Droplets of Prayer and Grace

1. "Ephesians 3:20-21 Commentary," *Precept Austin*, http://www.preceptaustin.org/ephesians_320-21.htm.

2. "140 Days of Prayer," *InTouch Ministries*, http://www.intouch.org/resources/140-days-of-prayer.

3. TerKeurst, Lysa, *Becoming More Than A Good Bible Study Girl* (Grand Rapids: Zondervan, 2009), 124.
4. Johnston, Julia and Towner, Daniel, "Grace Greater Than Our Sin," *Hymn Site,* http://www.hymnsite.com/lyrics/umh365.sht.
5. Young, Sarah, *Jesus Lives* (Nashville: Thomas Nelson, 2009*), 228-229.*
6. Newton, John, "Amazing Grace," *Constitution Society,* http://www.constitution.org/col/amazing_grace.htm